THE GIANT
PANDA

THE GIANT
PANDA

DAVID TAYLOR

Boxtree

First published in the UK 1990
by BOXTREE LIMITED, 36 Tavistock Street,
London WC2E 7PB

1 3 5 7 9 10 8 6 4 2

Text © David Taylor 1990

Illustrations © Boxtree Limited

Designed by Dave Goodman/Millions Design

Typeset in Bembo by Tradespools Ltd, Frome, Somerset

Colour reproduction by J. Film, Thailand

Printed and bound in Italy through OFSA

British Library Cataloguing in Publication Data
Taylor, David   1934-
      The Giant Panda.
      1. Pandas
      I. Title
      599.74443

      ISBN 1–85283–293–2

CONTENTS

To Andreas and Amanda

ACKNOWLEDGEMENTS

Many, many thanks to Penelope Cream, Elaine Collins and Cheryl Brown, my editors at Boxtree, and all the staff there; to José-Manuel Martos of Fotozoo, Zoo de la Casa de Campo, Madrid and John Knight, BVetMed, MRCVS, for their excellent photographs; to Dr. Tomas Cerdan and the Zoo de la Casa de Campo for the opportunity to work with 'Shao-Shao', 'Chang-Chang' and 'Chu-Lin' over the years and to my good veterinary *compañeros* in Madrid, Dr. Antonio-Luis Garcia del Campo and Dra. Liliana Monsalve.

INTRODUCTION

'big bear cat', the giant panda

Whoso walketh in solitude,
And inhabiteth the wood,
Choosing light, wave, rock and bird,
Before the money-loving herd,
Into that forester shall pass,
From these companions, power and grace.

RALPH WALDO EMERSON, *WOODNOTES*, PART II

What can one say about the giant panda, an animal as enigmatic and inscrutable as the people of its native China? It is famous and popular around the world, yet it is a mysterious, hermit-like character whose ways, whose very nature, are veiled in mists of fable and unknowing as elusive and ever-changing as the fogs that drift across the steep valleys and forest-clad slopes of Szechuan.

It has often been written that the giant panda was 'discovered' in 1869 by Père Armand David (1826–1900), a French missionary priest of the Order of St Vincent de Paul, when he came across a black and white pelt in the house of a rich landowner in Chengdu, the capital city of Szechuan.

Upon returning from an excursion we are invited to rest at the home of a certain Li, the principal landowner in the valley, who serves us tea and sweets. At this pagan's I see a fine skin of the famous black and white bear, which appears to be fairly large. It is a remarkable species and I am delighted when I hear my hunters say that I shall certainly obtain the animal within a short time. They tell me they will go out tomorrow to kill this animal, which will provide an interesting novelty for science.

FROM THE DIARY OF PÈRE DAVID

Although Père David was the first Westerner to learn of the existence of this creature, called '*pei-hsung*' (white bear) by the locals in the province of Szechuan, the Chinese people had known of the animal for many centuries before that and had prized it above all others.

Three thousand years before Père David's discovery, the first known collection of Chinese poetry, *The Book of Songs*, had referred to the giant

panda under the name 'pi'. Later, around the year 210 BC, a dictionary of the Qin dynasty gives the name '*mo*' to the animal, describing it as a white leopard with black markings, short legs and a predilection for eating copper, iron and bamboo. (Another black and white animal, the Malayan tapir, extinct in China since the 1850s, was also called '*mo*.') Somewhat confusingly, other ancient Chinese writings contain about twenty different names for the panda, some of which translate as 'bear-like cat', 'cat-like bear', 'great bear cat', 'patched bear' or 'monk bear'.

> *A bear-like, black and white animal that eats copper and iron lives in the Qionglai Mountains, south of Yandao County.*
>
> ANON, *SHAN-HAIJING, THE CLASSIC OF SEAS AND MOUNTAINS,* A CHINESE GEOGRAPHY BOOK OF 770 TO 256 BC

The giant panda's ancient reputation as a licker and eater of copper and iron may be based on the animal's undoubted tendency to lick any metal, such as dishes or cooking pots, that it might come across in the dwellings of Chinese peasants.

At the Zoo de la Casa de Campo, where the pandas receive their porridge of cooked rice, honey and yoghurt four times a day in stainless steel bowls, their metal-licking habit is plainly seen. Every scrap of food is ingested and then, holding the bowl in their two dextrous forepaws rather like the steering wheel of a car, they lick the metal meticulously clean while turning it round and round. The licking often continues for some time after all traces of porridge have gone and I wonder whether this behaviour is perhaps more a simple delight in the 'taste' of the steel than an instinctive search for trace elements, for their diet is carefully supplemented with all the minerals they need.

A skull of a giant panda (together with the skeleton of a rhinoceros, a species now extinct in China) has been unearthed from the burial pit near Xian of Bo, a Dowager Empress of the second century BC. An Eastern Han dictionary of the second century AD refers to 'Mo, who looks like a bear . . . lives in Szechuan . . . is of whitish colour, licks iron and can eat 10 *jing* (about 5 kg/11 lb) at one sitting . . . its fur is good for keeping you warm'. In the seventh century AD the Emperor Tang presented fourteen of his courtiers with panda pelts at a great banquet in Xian.

At the time of Père David's first description of the giant panda, French scientists concluded that it was a bear. The following year, it was decided that it was not a bear but a type of raccoon. Argument continues to this day over its classification, but it does seem that it is related to both the bears and the raccoons – and more especially to the charming lesser or red panda of the Himalayas.

The existence of the lesser or red panda (sometimes also known as the cat-bear), whose scientific name, *Ailurus fulgens*, means 'shining or gleaming cat', was first reported to the western world by a Frenchman, Frederic Cuvier (son of the illustrious zoologist, Baron Cuvier), 44 years before his

compatriot, Père David, found the giant panda. The Nepalese word for the lesser panda is 'nyalyaponga', and when the first live specimen arrived in London in the nineteenth century, the name was abbreviated and corrupted to 'panda'. The same name was later applied to Père David's new discovery.

Said to have a predilection for copper and iron, the giant panda does indeed seem to enjoy licking every scrap of food from its metal feeding bowl in the Madrid Zoo. (J.M. Martos)

> *I get a young chan-tche-cua or panda . . . the panda is an interesting animal already known in the Himalayas and formerly abundant in these forests, but now scarce . . . The Chinese call it 'child of the mountain' because its voice imitates that of a child.*
>
> *PÈRE DAVID WRITING ABOUT THE LESSER PANDA IN HIS DIARY,* 6 APRIL, 1869

Pandas may appear to have evolved out of nowhere around 3 million years ago. However, if we assume that they did not just materialize in a puff of smoke from Aladdin's lamp, what might their ancestors have been?

Some scientists believe that it all began with the American 'coon'. They postulate that some 6 to 10 million years ago raccoons from America migrated across the Bering Straits landbridge that then linked America and

Asia; that moving down from northern Asia, they gradually evolved into ancestors of the lesser panda; and that some settled in China and gave rise to the bigger, heavier giant panda.

A charming legend told by the peasants of central China, however, explains it another way. Once, long ago, so they say, pandas were completely white; the '*pei-hsung*' referred to earlier. A young girl befriended the animals and one day saved the life of a baby panda which was being attacked by a leopard. In doing so she was mortally wounded. When she died the giant pandas attended her funeral wearing black on their shoulders, arms and legs, the traditional Chinese signs of mourning. Moved to

Panda territory in the mountainous region of Szechuan contains a great variety of trees, shrubs and bamboo. Rainfall is quite light except during the long monsoon; constant dampness is provided by the shroud of mist and cloud. (J. Knight)

tears, the pandas wiped their eyes with their paws and turned them black. Then they held their heads in their paws, blackening their noses and ears. They have borne the marks of grief for their good friend ever since that day.

One of the fascinating aspects of the giant panda is that it seems always to have been quintessentially Chinese. Many animals that today are localized and 'exotic' were once much more widely distributed across the planet, for example elephant fossils have been dug up in England and Crete, and we know that lions roamed south-eastern Europe up until the time of Christ. Fossil pandas, on the other hand, have been found *only* in

China, with one exception, in Burma. Though now restricted to montane forests in parts of central China, they once lived right across the eastern part of the country. A reported sighting (at a distance of over 3 km/1³/₄ miles) of a female giant panda and two cubs walking in open country in north-eastern Tibet on a June morning in 1940 is now thought to have been mistaken. The trio, with the cubs suckling from their mother as she foraged, were more likely brown bears.

The lesser panda on the other hand is still more widely distributed. Although sparsely scattered, one sub-species is still found in the Himalayas from Nepal to Assam, and the other in parts of China and northern

The lesser panda, or 'child of the mountains', is a good climber, being light and nimble. (J.M. Martos)

Burma. It inhabits the bamboo forest above an altitude of 1,500 m (4,920 ft), and in a few places its haunts overlap with those of its giant namesake.

The giant panda's appeal

The strong appeal of the giant panda to human beings arises not so much in its status as a rare and reclusive zoological curiosity, as in its teddy-bear appearance, enhanced by its striking coat markings. The human psyche reacts instinctively and particularly towards faces that present, *or appear to present*, large eyes. Tiny babies will smile at a piece of paper on which a circle with two black discs has been drawn, ladies used belladonna drops in days gone by to expand their pupils and create the illusion of big eyes, and much of the attraction of Mickey Mouse lies in the way his eyes are drawn, big and dark. The black patches around the giant panda's eyes magnify this attractive feature and people instantly warm to them.

Sadly, although they might look like it, giant pandas are *not* cuddly teddy-bears. Their fur is rather coarse and greasy and, as I know to my cost, cuddling them can be exceedingly dangerous, for they are powerful individuals with a strong grip, hard claws and a formidable bite.

From hunting trophy to protected species

Early in the twentieth century a number of expeditions from the West went in search of the giant panda. Theodore and Kermit Roosevelt had the dubious honour of being the first to shoot an adult panda, in April 1929. However, the current popular concern for the conservation of endangered wildlife species and the particular threat to pandas in modern times posed by the flowering and subsequent dying-off of the bamboo on which they rely, have made the world at large very conscious of the panda's plight.

> *Our great good fortune could only with much effort be credited. After holding aloof, the Hunting Gods had turned about and brewed the unusual chain of circumstances that alone could enable us to shoot a giant panda, trailing him without dogs and with the crowning bit of luck that permitted us to fire jointly.*
>
> THEODORE & KERMIT ROOSEVELT, *TRAILING THE GIANT PANDA* (1929)

In 1937, the first live specimen, a male, to be captured and brought to a Western zoo arrived at Brookfield Zoo, Chicago. A year later a female, 'Pandora', arrived in New York, and five pandas, three males and two females, were sent to London. Moscow was presented with its first panda in 1955, and Japan, France, West Germany, the USA (Washington), Mexico, Spain and North Korea also received pandas as the years went by.

The first Chinese zoo to keep giant pandas was that of Chengdu in Szechuan, which obtained its first animal in 1953. Beijing Zoo acquired three young pandas in 1955, and the first giant panda birth in captivity occurred there on 9 September, 1963.

In their early days in zoos, giant pandas were, in many cases, little more than part of the menagerie, a spectacular crowd-pulling sideshow. Just

President Theodore Roosevelt and his four sons: Theodore, jr., and Archibald are seated on the president's right, while Quentin (the baby) and Kermit occupy the left. Theodore, jr. and Kermit were among the first Western hunters to track and kill the giant panda. Fortunately, in later years, fears for the future of the panda meant that hunting and trapping were severely restricted. (Mary Evans Picture Library).

before the outbreak of World War II, a male panda called 'Happy' toured German zoos; and in 1958 'Chi-Chi the Second' did the rounds of Moscow, Berlin, Frankfurt and Copenhagen. Trained pandas have even appeared riding bicycles and performing other tricks from the old 'dancing bear' repertoires of Chinese circuses.

Thankfully the considerable commercial value of giant pandas as showbiz stars is no longer the pre-eminent reason for their presence in a select handful of zoological collections; the role of zoos in the scientific study and conservation of these animals is growing. Captive breeding, including experiments in artificial insemination, is increasingly successful. Research projects are also undertaken on pandas in the wild, such as that carried out by a joint Chinese-American team at the Wolong Nature Reserve. They are providing a wealth of invaluable information on the ways of the species, which will help to ensure its survival.

The hunting of giant pandas is now prohibited by the Chinese government on pain of death, and strict laws are in force for their protection. Nonetheless, cured panda skins are still occasionally offered for sale in Hong Kong and Taiwan, and there are those in Pakistan who claim they are willing to smuggle live pandas out of China, dyed brown in the hope that they might pass as brown bears, for the right price.

The sublime Changbai Mountains, the breathtakingly beautiful Wuyi Mountains, the lush tropical scenery of Xishuangbanna, the Elysioan springs and forests of Jiuzhaigou, the much loved giant panda in groves of brilliant green bamboo, Bird Island, a star in Quinghai Lake, the mysterious Isle of Snakes, a group of fourteen volcanoes at five Joined Lakes. Here is Nature in all her glory . . . Sixty-eight of China's animal species are at the first level of national protection, including the giant panda, crested ibis . . . golden monkey, takin, Indian elephant, Indian bison, two-humped camel, Przewalski's horse, Chinese river dolphin, red-crowned crane, Siberian crane, brown-eared pheasant and Chinese alligator.

LI WENHUA AND ZHAO XIANYING, *CHINA'S NATURE RESERVES*

Apart from the handsome pelt, other parts of the 'black and white bear's' body were highly prized in traditional Chinese medicine. These included the paws, fat and, especially, the gall bladder. Bears of all kinds were reputed never to fall ill on account of their gall-bladders which were believed efficiently to 'detoxify' anything eaten by the animal. Thus ground dried bear gall was, and is in many parts of the Orient, considered to make a powerful panacea and tonic for human beings.

There are no figures for the number of pandas in the wild today. A census carried out between 1974 and 1977 suggested a total of just over 1000, but the widespread flowering and death of bamboo between 1974 and 1976 caused a sharp decline in the numbers of pandas in some areas, a decline that was not included in the census figures. There have been more recent bamboo flowerings, again with pandas dying of starvation, and it may well be the case that at this time only 500 to 1,000 of the animals remain.

This is the story of the remarkable and intriguing creatures that make up that fragile population.

WHAT IS

THE PANDA?

The giant panda . . . is classified as an aberrant bear.
ENCYCLOPAEDIA BRITANNICA

'But I do beguile the thing I am by seeming otherwise.' The words of Shakespeare's Othello seem ever to be appropriate to the giant panda. The question is simple: in zoological terms, what is the giant panda? Since 1869, when Père Armand David first admired the beautiful black and white pelt hanging in the landowner's house in Chengdu, scientists have argued over the animal's correct classification. Its original scientific name, *Ursus melanoleucus* (black and white bear), given in the year of Père David's discovery, placed it firmly in the Ursidae (bear) family. The creature looked like a black and white cousin of the Himalayan black bear, the sun bear and the sloth bear, all natives of Asia. However, in 1870 anatomists decided that it was not a bear but a member of the raccoon family, and re-christened it *Ailuropoda melanoleuca* (black and white foot), a name that it still retains. The raccoon family, the Procyonidae, includes, as well as six species of raccoon, creatures like the ringtail, cacomistle, kinkajou, olingo and coati – all native to the Americas and, with the exception of the kinkajou, possessing dark rings on their tails.

Later that year other experts disagreed again, it *was* a sort of bear. By 1885 it was a raccoon-type again, and in 1913 it was back among the bears. Studies in 1964 concluded that it was indeed a raccoon, but 15 years later other studies plumped yet again for its being a bear. There have been numerous other changes of mind on the matter, and if a panda could read the many learned papers on the subject, it would undoubtedly develop acute schizophrenia, for roughly half the experts over the years have put their money on the panda being a bear while the other half back it as a raccoon.

What, then, is the evidence available to the panda genealogist? Is the lesser or red panda the giant panda's closest living relative? Is the giant panda more of a raccoon and less of a bear, or the reverse? Or is it, perhaps, completely unique?

The giant panda is a moderate climber, and appears quite happy to remain amongst the branches of a tree for some time. (J.M. Martos)

For and against the raccoon theory
Most experts are now agreed that the lesser panda and the giant panda are descended from a common ancestor, and are therefore quite closely

A young raccoon afloat on a log in Wyoming, North America. The raccoon has many features which are similar to those of the lesser panda. The most striking of these are the ringed tail and the circled eyes. (Survival Anglia/Des and Jen Bartlett)

A lesser panda in the wild, displaying the ringed tail. (J. Knight)

related. Because the lesser panda is very raccoon-like in shape and size, and has a ringed tail, many zoologists have judged it to be a procyonid whose thumbs and teeth in particular have become specialized for eating rough plant material. Those who subscribe to the raccoon theory point out that if the lesser panda is a type of raccoon, and if the lesser and giant pandas are

The Himalayan black bear, also known as the 'moon bear' because of the crescent-shaped marking on its chest. (Bruce Coleman/Gerald Cubitt)

closely related, the giant panda must be a type of raccoon too. They make much of physical and behavioural resemblances between the pandas and the procyonids, such as skull and teeth design, scent-marking habits, vocalization, and the number of chromosomes in the nuclei of their body cells.

In addition, the alimentary canal of the pandas is much shorter than one would expect to find in a descendant of the bear, whose guts are quite long. If the pandas were bears that switched to dedicated vegetarianism, why would they evolve a shorter gut, quite the opposite of what seems essential in an animal faced with the problem of digesting plant fibre?

The fact that all other living procyonids are American species does not necessarily contradict this theory as fossil evidence shows that procyonids did once live in Europe and Asia.

For and against the bear theory

Unlike the lesser panda, the giant panda looks like a bear. In many languages it is even called a bear. Its pigeon-toed walk, swinging from side to side with head held low, is like that of a bear. The giant panda's skeleton, however, is much heavier than the bear's, and this is reflected in its lumbering, slower and less agile movements. Although the development of a heavy skull to withstand the crunching of bamboo would be a logical evolutionary modification, why should the whole skeleton become so unbearlike and clumsy? Maybe to bludgeon its way through dense bamboo. More likely, however, is that its ponderous skeleton developed as a result of the rapid enlargement of its body after it had become a bamboo addict, and most experts now agree on the likelihood that the giant panda was originally a bamboo-eating animal that grew big, rather than a big animal that took to eating bamboo.

Several parts of the internal anatomy of the giant panda – the brain, ears, musculature and respiratory system for example – are very bear-like, and modern analysis of the blood proteins, including DNA 'finger-printing', suggest that both the giant and lesser pandas are closer to the bears than to the raccoons.

This latter line of research, however, goes on to tantalize us further by hinting that the giant panda may be closer to the Himalayan black bear than to the lesser panda; and that, flying in the face of orthodox palaeontological opinion, bears are themselves an offshoot of the raccoon family rather than of the dog family, as previously supposed. If that were the case, it would allow us to draw up a very convenient family tree, and one which might fit in with the theory of the panda's early ancestors being a sort of raccoon that migrated via a land-bridge from North America to Europe and Asia. However, the fossil records, as currently interpreted, do not support this theory.

In the light of current knowledge, and while the scientific evidence does not conclusively fall one way or the other, we can safely say that the two pandas are probably more closely related to one another than to any other species, and that beyond that, they are nearer to bears than racoons, while sharing a common ancestry with both.

The giant panda's bearish appearance may be an example of convergent evolution, when an animal grows to look like another species to which it is not closely related. As the zoologist Desmond Morris has written, perhaps the giant panda is a 'fake bear'. There are many examples of convergent evolution – the harmless flies that mimic wasps, the dolphins which with their streamlined bodies and fin-like flippers, at first sight resemble fish, and the many kinds of marsupial in Australia which, though they have made a different evolutionary journey over millions of years, are so similar in many aspects of form and function to unrelated mammals on other continents.

Fossil records

The fossil records give few clues to the lineage of the pandas. Fossils of a 12 million year old proto lesser panda have been discovered in Europe and North America. This animal appears to have survived in the European forests until about 1 million years ago, long after the procyonids which once inhabited the region had vanished. A small bear-like animal also lived in Europe about 20 million years ago and, by virtue of its tooth structure, might have been an ancestor of the giant panda.

Fossils of the two pandas, much in the form that we know them, have

Miacis, ancestor of so many carnivorous animals, including the hyaena, mongoose, weasel, bear and raccoon.

been found in China, the oldest dating back between 1 and 2 million years. The earliest fossil giant panda so far unearthed is that of a small creature weighing about half as much as the modern animal – more evidence, perhaps, that the giant panda began small and grew in size after converting to a bamboo diet.

A likely evolution

The panda's ancestry is still a puzzle. From the often-conflicting evidence, we can draw up a picture of the likely evolution of the panda, but we can only guess at parts of it.

By the late Cretaceous period, 65 million years ago, when the last of the dinosaurs were on the brink of becoming extinct, the first mammals had already existed for a long time. They were small, long-nosed, insect-eating creatures, probably similar in appearance to the solenodon, a shrew-like animal that still lives in parts of Cuba and Haiti. Some of the early mammals remained as small insectivores; some evolved into herbivores and became the ancestors of the ungulates – the hoofed animals alive today. A third group developed into the first carnivores: small mammals with long bodies, short limbs, clawed feet and tiny brains, called creodonts.

The creodonts in turn evolved into a wide variety of predatory animals, some as big as wolves and lions, but all of them were extinct by the start of the Pliocene period some 12 million years ago. Before they disappeared, however, one of the earliest creodonts had evolved into a new and very important group of creatures, the miacids. Still small and forest-dwelling, the miacids had a trump card in the survival game – they had much bigger brains than the dim creodonts. These bright little meat-eaters were the stock from which all present-day carnivores sprang, not just the cat and

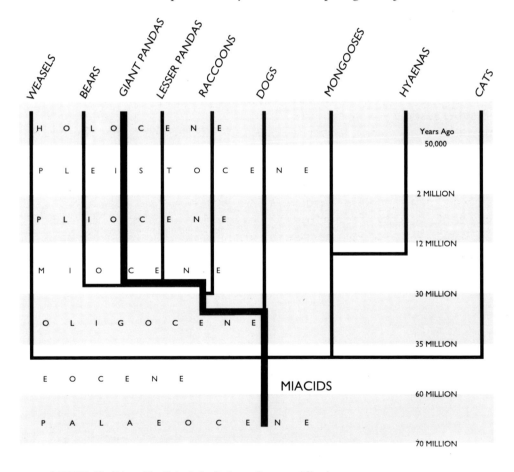

NOTES: The Weasel family includes Badgers, Otters and Skunks
The Raccoon family includes Coatis, Kinka jous and Cacomistles
The Mongoose family includes Civets, Genets and Fossas

dog families, but also the hyaenas, mongooses, weasels, bears and raccoons.

Exactly when the miacids began to develop into separate carnivore families can only be roughly guessed at. By the late Eocene period, 36 million years ago, four main branches of the carnivora can be recognized in the fossil record – the cats, dogs, mongooses and weasels. Around 30 million years ago the raccoons split off from the dogs, and then perhaps 6 million years later the pandas arose as another spur from the dog line, shortly followed by the bears. Still fairly small carnivores, the pandas found themselves in, or were forced into, an unoccupied biological niche in the bamboo forests of China. Switching gradually to a vegetarian diet, they developed into the lesser and giant pandas of modern times.

In the Pleistocene epoch 3 to 1 million years ago the giant panda's homeland extended right across eastern China, almost as far north as Beijing and south into Burma and the Nanling mountain range that stretched from south-eastern Kweichow to northern Kwangtung. However, the western highlands centred on Szechuan became its securest stronghold, for when the glaciers of the north began to expand during the Pleistocene ice age, the pandas and some other unusual animal species survived, not least because they were protected from an invasion of mammals from the north by the formidable barriers created by the deserts of the Gobi and central Asia.

Notwithstanding the doubts and debates that surround them, the two pandas, lesser and greater, are still frequently classified in zoology books as procyonids, paid-up members of the raccoon family. However, an increasing number of zoologists are now in favour of either giving each of the pandas its own separate though closely related family, or of putting them in a family of their own, to be called the Ailuropodidae or Ailuridae.

2

THE PHYSICAL CHARACTERISTICS OF THE PANDA

少所見多所怪

'The less a man has seen, the more he has to wonder at.' Chinese proverb

I am tired of being told there is no such animal by animals who are merely different.

D.H. LAWRENCE
(IN A LETTER TO J.M. MURRAY)

When Père David first saw the giant panda skin he must already have heard of the animal's existence, for he referred to it in his diary for that day as '*le fameaux ours blanc et noir*', the *famous* black and white bear. Less than two weeks later he was brought the corpse of a 'young white bear' by hunters, and lost no time in writing home to Paris with an initial description of his find. The 'bear', he wrote, was 'very large'.

Large, however, the giant panda is not, especially when compared to commoner, true bears such as the brown bear, which can weigh over 400 kg (800 lb) with a head to tail-tip length of almost 3 m (10 ft), or even the Himalayan black bear, the males of which can measure 1.8 km (6 ft) long and tip the scales at 180 kg (400 lb).

My immediate impression on seeing a live giant panda for the first time, like many people's, was that it was much smaller than I had imagined from written descriptions and illustrations. Adult giant panda males, somewhat bigger than the females, rarely exceed 1.5 m (5 ft) in length, and although they can weigh up to 150 kg (330 lb), they are usually much closer to 110 kg (245 lb). It is a 'giant' only when compared against its putative cousin, the lesser panda.

The lesser panda resembles a red-coated raccoon, though with a rounder, less pointed head. It weighs 3–4.5 kg ($7^3/_4$–$8^3/_4$ lb) and measures 80–110 cm ($31^1/_2$–$43^1/_2$ in) long with a tail of 29–50 cm (11–$19^3/_4$ in), against the raccoon's 5–12 kg (11–$26^1/_2$ lb), and length of 60–100 cm ($23^1/_2$–$39^1/_2$ in) and tail of 20–40 cm ($7^3/_4$–$15^3/_4$ in).

The eyes of the giant panda appear to be larger than they really are because of the black markings around them. (Bruce Coleman/ WWF/Kojo Tanaka)

The lesser panda

The lesser panda is a secretive, mainly nocturnal creature about whose life-style we know very little. It, too, leads a solitary existence within a personal territory, the boundaries of which it scent marks.

It is a much better climber than the giant panda and spends much of its time up in the trees either foraging for food or napping comfortably, like a cat, in the fork of a branch. Though well-protected by its fur and indifferent to cold and drizzle, it seeks shelter from the wind and rain, and is distinctly uncomfortable in warm weather.

Although shy and diffident at first meeting, the lesser panda is at heart an amenable creature, full of curiosity and delighting in play, particularly when young. I have found the cubs as boisterous as puppies, loving to stand up on their hind legs and box my hands. The animal tames quite easily and was, at one time, popular as an exotic pet (thankfully they are seldom found in this role any more). It isn't very vocal, but will sometimes emit weak squeaks, chirps or short whistles. When harassed it will often spit or hiss and at the same time may expel an acrid-smelling secretion from its anal sacs.

A female brown bear and cubs fishing in fast-moving water. Pandas are also competent swimmers if put to it. (Survival Anglia/Jeff Foott)

A rare close-up of the very shy lesser panda, showing in detail its facial characteristics. (J.M. Martos)

Stocky and squat, with short, stout legs, a generous paunch, broad, rather squared-off buttocks and a small stub of a tail, the giant panda has an unathletic appearance. The fluffy-looking coat, the striking patches of black and white (actually off-white to cream), and the appealing facial markings, combined with the rolling gait, solitary life-style, and preference for napping over physical exertion, create an image of a peaceable, bucolic character.

The coat of the giant panda is dense and only slightly fluffy with hair of moderate length; to the touch it feels neither lush or wooly, but rather greasy. The skin glands secrete plenty of oil to keep the loose-packed hairs comfortably rain-proof – an essential requirement in the western highlands of China. The coat of the lesser panda is bright chestnut in colour, and thick and lush, on the upper part of the body, while the legs and underside are darker, often almost black.

The familiar, sharply delineated black and white markings of the giant panda's coat (all pandas display the same design) pose the interesting ques-

As can be seen here, the giant panda has a short 'paint brush' of a tail. (Bruce Coleman/ WWF/Kojo Tanaka)

tion: to what purpose? Why evolve so bold a harlequin costume?

In other black and white species, the skin or coat colouration serves a variety of useful purposes. In zebras the striping probably acts as a sort of banner enabling individuals to see one another easily and keep together, reinforcing herd cohesion. Also, under the glare of the African sun a group of zebra create a jazzy effect of black and white bands that may confuse predators. Marine mammals, such as some dolphins and the killer whale, are black and white, with more black on the upper surface of the body and more white beneath. This is camouflage at work: if you look down on the animal with the light behind you, or up at it framed against the sunlight, the animal merges with the background. Such camouflage serves as a protection against predators for the dolphin, and to conceal the predator itself in the case of the killer whale.

The black and white plumage of a bird like the magpie is not for camouflage; quite the reverse. The distinctive flashes of white against black aid mutual recognition and play a vital role in the mating rituals. Black and white markings on moving parts of the body – the tails of ring-tailed lemurs, or the backs of the ears of tigers – serve as a means of visual communication, particularly with offspring.

The striking markings of animals like the skunk serve as a warning to potential enemies.

So what about our black and white 'harlequin bear'? Its colouring could provide a degree of camouflage in open spaces covered with snow, such as the high mountain zones in winter, but these are rarely visited by the

Snowy conditions present no problem to the giant panda; its extremely dense coat allows it to withstand both cold and damp with ease. (Rex Features)

panda, and in the bamboo forests it stands out very obviously. The occasional leopard or marauding pack of red dogs may pose a threat once in a while, but the panda's life is essentially not a high-risk one, and it does not need camouflage to stalk bamboo. And, living a quiet rather parochial and lonely life, it doesn't have much need for visual communication.

The giant panda's colours stand out so starkly against the foliage that it is safe to assume it 'wants' to be seen. Unless, but this is most unlikely, it is one of Mother Nature's incorrigible dandies who takes a vain delight in showing off to the rest of creation. However, evolution does not work like that. The panda's costume is probably designed, like that of the skunk, as a warning to the occasional predator – clouded leopard, Himalayan bear or red dog – giving off a message such as: 'Don't think I'm an easy mark, a lumbering, slow-witted, *unarmed* vegetarian – because I'm not.' And that's the truth, as I know to my cost. The panda is an immensely strong beast with a bite as powerful as that of a grizzly bear; it has to be to slice those rigid bamboo stems.

Having wrestled in earnest with a half-grown giant panda and been bitten by it – in play – and finding it frighteningly impossible to break the grip of those six-clawed paws, I can well imagine the damage an angry adult panda could inflict. Fang teeth flashing as it curls its trunk to protect its underbelly, reaching out with those heavy forearms and iron-hard claws, its dense coat and tight skin give little to grab hold of. A sensible bear wouldn't tangle with such a fellow; a prudent leopard is best advised to look for a wild pig or deer.

At least twice a year I have the opportunity to examine in detail the teeth of a giant panda when, at the Zoo de la Casa de Campo in Madrid, Spain, I tranquillize the old male 'Chang-Chang' or his step-son 'Chu-Lin', and use an ultrasonic descaler to remove the deposits of hard, calcified tartar which build up on the tooth enamel and threaten the gum margins with gingivitis.

A giant panda in typical bamboo-crunching pose; the stem is being held in the paw and is steadily chewed from the side of the mouth. (Bruce Coleman/WWF/Timm Rautert)

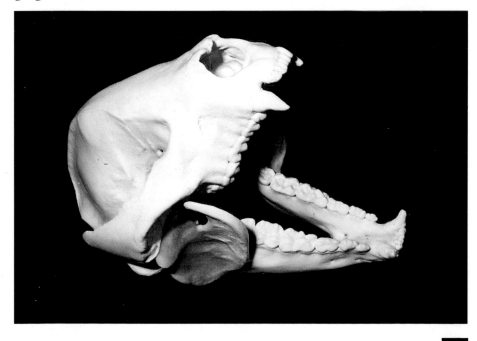

The skull of the giant panda showing the modified dentition adapted for effective chewing of bamboo. (J.M. Martos)

The teeth of the giant panda are, in most respects, quite unlike those of grazing and browsing herbivores such as deer or giraffes. With three incisors (front teeth), one large canine (fang tooth) and five or six pre-molars and molars (cheek teeth) top and bottom on both sides of the jaw, the dentition is, at first sight, that of a carnivore. Closer inspection shows that the teeth, while based on a standard carnivore model which gives away the panda's meat-eating ancestry, have become modified over the ages for the mastication of bamboo. Most of the cheek teeth are broad and have strong points and ridges. They are powerful grindstones, similar in some ways to the cheek teeth of pigs, with more grinding surface than those of bears, and far less emphasis on the slicing and shearing functions so prominent in the teeth of the cat and dog families. The teeth of the lesser panda are much the same as those of its giant relative. To accommodate the grindstone teeth and the enlarged muscles which power the bite and chewing movements, the skulls of both pandas have become broader compared to those of bears, and in order to anchor the musculature firmly, the skull bones are thick and heavy.

The giant panda's eyes are dark and round. The black ring of fur around the eyes creates the illusion of a face with enormous eyes, but in fact they are not very big. The pupil of the panda's eye, like that of the cat, is a vertical slit. This seems to indicate that the animal's retina is particularly sensitive to light. Slit pupils can contract more completely than circular, human-type ones, and thereby protect the retina better in bright conditions. Perhaps this enables the panda to cope effectively with snow glare, and to see in low light levels during night time when adults continue to forage for food.

The most famous and unique anatomical feature of the panda is its extra or sixth digit on each forepaw, the curious thumb that gives it a high degree of dexterity and particularly a firm grasp of the bamboo cane. Both the giant panda and the lesser panda (which possesses a smaller version of the same structure) can, in the manner of man and other primates, oppose the special thumb against the first digit, something which no bear can do.

All mammal paws are built to a basic pattern of five digits (toes or fingers). During the process of evolution certain animals have lost or dispensed with some of the digits. The dog has four toes plus a remnant of the fifth, called a dew-claw. In the horse the process has gone further, the toes being reduced to one, with the nail or claw having developed into the hoof. The splint bones are remnants of the other digits. But no species apart from the pandas have increased the basic number of digits because evolutionary laws do not permit additions. Occasionally, *individuals* of a species may, by chance, be born with more than the usual number of digits. Cases of humans with as many as seven or eight fingers or toes on each limb have been recorded, such supernumerary digits being emblematic of great wisdom or royal birth to certain ancient peoples like the Chaldeans. However, these are rare congenital conditions. Yet the panda's extra thumb is no freak happening or rare mutation; is it *normal* anatomy.

The panda's extra thumb does not in fact break the basic 'five-toe' design of mammalian evolution, for it is not a true additional digit but a

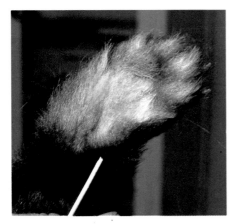

The lesser panda also has an especially dextrous 'extra' thumb, which forms the sixth digit. (J. Knight)

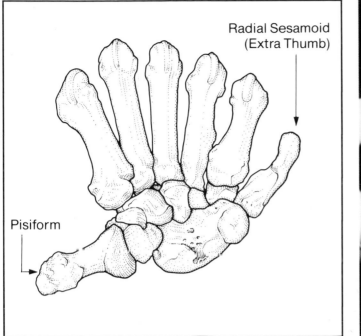

Radial Sesamoid
(Extra Thumb)

Pisiform

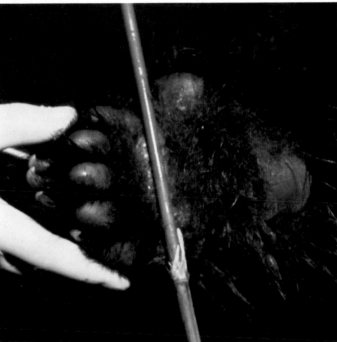

The unusual sixth digit on a giant panda's paw is here demonstrated gripping a bamboo stem. (J. Knight)

'fake' one that lacks a claw. It arose as a pronounced outward elongation of the radial sesamoid, one of the collection of knobbly little bones that make up the wrist joint. It can be moved independently of the true digits and is operated by four strong muscles. When I have anaesthetized a giant panda, one of the signs I continually check as the animal comes round is the grip of the extra thumb on one of my fingers. When it clenches tight and I have to pull hard to free myself, I know my patient will be fully conscious within a few minutes.

Another bone, the pisiform, on the opposite side of the wrist is also un-usually long, and it has been suggested that this, too, may be able to move and assist the panda in grasping the bamboo by acting as a *seventh* digit.

The digestive system of the giant panda is surprisingly simple for an animal which feeds almost exclusively on fibrous vegetable food. There is no long alimentary tract, multi-chambered stomach or large caecum and colon characteristic of herbivores.

The giant panda's alimentary tract has a single-chambered stomach like that of a human or dog, but with a large, very muscular pyloric portion (next to the duodenum), which has been described as 'gizzard-like'. In the course of examining the stomachs of living pandas by means of a fibre-optic endoscope, I cannot say that I have seen much resemblance to the gizzard of a bird, nor have I encountered the 'horny' lining of the gullet (oesophagus) that has also been mentioned in the past. However, I have seen large quantities of coarsely chopped bamboo lying in the stomach, in pieces of a length and thickness that suggest the panda does not follow William Ewart Gladstone's stern Victorian precept of chewing food thirty-six times before swallowing. Somehow the mucous membrane lin-ing the stomach, protected only by the copious liquid it secretes, with-stands the regular delivery of supplies of this rough-cut timber.

Beyond the stomach the gut is short, though a much higher proportion of its length is taken up by large, rather than small, intestine. The reverse situation is to be found in the dog, whose gut length in comparison to body length is about the same as in the panda. The intestines of the panda and the dog are about five times the length of their bodies, whereas the intestines of a herbivore such as the cow is about twenty times its body length.

All in all, it seems that the panda didn't evolve any anatomical adaptations of the alimentary tract when it became a bamboo specialist, except for the unusually high number of mucus-producing glands in the intestinal wall.

The scent-marking of objects is a common feature of panda behaviour. On each side of the panda's anus there is a small gland, or anal sac, similar to that which causes such frequent irritation in dogs. Raccoons and other procyonids also possess anal sacs, but in the bear they are poorly developed or completely absent. The sacs secrete a thin liquid which, to the human nose, has a rather sharp, vinegary odour. The skin immediately surrounding the anus and genitals is hairless with many creases containing more microscopic glands. This smell-producing ano-genital area is covered by the stubby tail which, when lifted, helps to apply the glandular secretions to anything against which the bottom is rubbed during marking. The lesser panda has a similar pair of well-developed anal sacs and a naked, creased area around the anus.

Another un-bearlike part of the anatomy is the penis of both the giant and lesser panda. Whereas in bears the organ is long, straight and pointed forward like that of a dog, in the panda it is much smaller than might be expected, S-shaped and directed backwards as in the cat (fireside tom and African lion).

Like the bears, however, the giant panda's kidney is lobulated; it is composed of a mulberry-shaped agglomeration of, usually, six separate small kidney units. It looks like a smaller version of the cow's kidney regularly on display in the butcher's window. Among carnivores, the Polar bear has the highest number of kidney lobules – around sixty-five. The lesser panda kidney is not lobulated and more resembles that of the cat, dog or human being.

Although shy and retiring, the lesser panda is playful and inquisitive. (J.M. Martos)

3

THE HOME

OF THE

PANDA

Far in a wild, unknown to public view
From youth to age a reverend hermit grew
The moss his bed, the cave his humble cell,
His food the fruits, his drink the crystal well.

THOMAS PARNELL, *THE HERMIT*

The giant panda is now restricted to bamboo forest on the slopes of six mountainous regions in the western highlands of China that lie within the provinces of Szechuan, Kansu and Shensi. At the heart of this part of China is an area known as the Red Basin, a plateau that, 300 million years ago, was submerged under the sea; 150 million years later, it became a freshwater lake. A sediment of red sand gradually accumulated in the lake, forming the present wrinkled, ochre-coloured terrain and giving it its name. To the west of the Basin is the immense eastern Tibetan fault line where the earth's crust has been restless for aeons and has thrust up a mighty palisade of mountains, most of which are well over 400 m (13,000 ft) high, and in whose gorges the first tributaries of China's longest river, the Yangtze Kiang, rise. Beyond lies the bleak plateau of Tibet.

To the north of the Red Basin, another lower but still great range of mountains, the Chin Ling Shan, runs east-west just south of Xian, the provincial capital of Shensi, and points a finger towards Shanghai 700 km (435 miles) away. On the slopes of these mountains, running down via broad terraces towards the Red Basin, are the six isolated areas of giant panda country – the only ones now remaining. The smallest covers about 30,000 hectares (74,000 acres), the biggest perhaps 1.3 million hectares (7.4 million acres), but it is important to realize that they include many zones that are not suitable habitat for the animal – high alpine land, ravines, steep slopes, rivers, rhododendron forest, and land cultivated by man. The only part that is of practical use to the giant pandas is the bamboo forest found at an altitude of 1,200 to 3,500 m (3,940–11,500 ft), and of that there is at present perhaps no more than $^1/_2$ million hectares (1.2 million acres).

A giant panda surveys the surrounding terrain from its perch. (Rex Features)

This map illustrates the area inhabited by
the panda today and the regions where it is
believed pandas once lived in earlier times,
often where fossils have been found. The
dramatic reduction in area is an indication of
the need for conservation today.

Area of Prehistoric Finds

Present Panda Range

The varied mountain habitat contains both fast-flowing rivers and a wide assortment of trees and bamboo thickets. (J. Knight)

The lesser panda has a wider distribution. Although sparsely scattered, one sub-species is still found in the Himalayas from Nepal to Assam, and the other in parts of China and northern Burma. It inhabits the bamboo forest above an altitude of 1,500 m (4,920 ft), and in a few places its haunts overlap with those of its giant namesake.

The lowlands of the Red Basin, in Szechuan in particular, has rich soil and a mild climate, winters that are not too cold and summer monsoons. The area is ideal for growing rice and cereals as well as sugar, hemp, mulberries, oranges, maize and tobacco. Szechuan is famous for its luscious apples and peaches, and its landscape is rich in colourful flowers. Until the last millenium BC this area was under Indian rule and evidence of Indian influences still persist – the cultivation of sugar cane, the use of great water-wheels for irrigation and the presence in the fields of water buffalo and zebu cattle.

The bottom of this valley is quite high and is surrounded by mountains that are wooded on the upper parts. The atmosphere is humid and it rains and snows frequently. The vegetation is abundant here because of the many streams and springs, one of which flows under the floor of my room. Among the trees I notice many magnificent conifers, such as Keteleeria with trunks rising to a great height before branching out, and crowned with an elegant dark-green pyramidal top.

THE DIARY OF PÈRE DAVID

The western highlands

The mountains of the western highlands that flank the Basin are remote, inaccessible and stunningly beautiful. The steep sides of deep cleft gorges reach down to fast-running rivers and furious rapids. Above, the often precipitous valley walls are closely clad with trees. On the lower slopes vine-embraced stands of beech, birch, cinnamon, laurel, cherry and evergreen oak are interspersed with bamboo. On some of the broader valley bottoms, and even on some higher slopes, there are small farms surrounded by fields. Higher up, between 1,500 and 2,000 m (4,920–6,560 ft) there are birches, maples, lacquer trees, filberts, willows, walnuts and dense bamboo thickets. In some places the dove tree, native only to China, grows in vast forests. Higher still one finds more conifers – spruce, fir, and larch – and birch, cherry and alder, again mixed with masses of bamboo. Ascending still further into the main feeding range of the giant panda, between 2,500 and 3,500 m (8,200–11,500 ft), many different species of rhododendron are in evidence alongside the bamboo, birch and firs. Above 3,500 m (11,500 ft) there is no more bamboo, just rhododendron, dwarf junipers and firs, which thin out and at last disappear where the grassy alps begin. These steep meadows are carpeted in late spring and summer with a profusion of gentians, Chinese globeflowers, golden rays, primroses, orchids and ragworts.

The climate of the western highlands is characterized by cold, snowy winters that last about five months, although the temperature rarely drops below −10°C (14°F), rainy springs and cool, humid, early summers. In June, the monsoon sweeps across unimpeded from the Pacific, and when checked by the high mountain barrier it creates a moist atmosphere over the mountains, ensuring drizzly weather for much of late summer and autumn. Consequently, panda paradise consists of fog, rain or snow, or a combination of all three, and a bed of dripping bamboo loaded with young shoots and shrouded in mist.

> *Nature rarely speaks*
> *Hence the whirlwind does not last a whole morning*
> *Nor the sudden rainstorm last a whole day.*
> *What causes this?*
> *If Heaven and Earth cannot make them long lasting,*
> *How much less so can humans?*
>
> LAO SE, *TAO-TE-CHING*

The bamboo forest

Though intermingled with other trees and shrubs, and broken in places by more open areas of bushy undergrowth, the bamboo mainly grows in tightly packed thickets which are virtually impenetrable by man. Pandas, on the other hand, move through it with ease, using well-worn trails and dark gloomy tunnels that they have driven through the vegetation with their strong, stocky bodies.

Mist is an almost constant characteristic of panda terrain; the moisture provides a fertile climate for growth of vegetation, including the various flowering shrubs, such as this flourishing rhododendron. (J. Knight)

It has been calculated that far more bamboo still exists in panda country than is needed to support present numbers of the species. Every square kilometre (one-third of a square mile) of good bamboo forest in the western highlands can provide sustenance for one to two pandas, so theoretically the total panda habitat could support a population of 6,000 pandas or more. However, other factors also need to be considered.

It seems certain that the giant panda existed for many thousands of years with little competition from other species and with very few significant

predators. In days gone by man hunted the pandas for their skins, but to no serious extent because the natural haunts of the creature were too remote and inhospitable. However, when man unwittingly began to modify the habitat of the panda the decline in numbers began in earnest, and the position today is that the animals cling on precariously within their last redoubts.

Even the wildest places, once so difficult of access, have been slowly but persistently invaded by man and his technology. Roads have brought settlements and farms. The settlements have been accompanied by the logging of other tree species that grow among the bamboo. Farming has expanded, particularly in the broader valleys, fields of wheat, barley, millet, beans and vegetables replacing trees on the mountain slopes, often to an altitude of 200 m (6,560 ft) or more. The local inhabitants have for a long time visited the edges of the bamboo forest to collect firewood and timber for building. As a result, in many places the lower limits of the bamboo growth has been driven steadily upwards.

There is no doubt that up to the present time the principal, even the only enemy of the panda has been *Homo sapiens*. Today, the status of the bamboo forest itself, particularly with regard to man's influence on it, the isolation of the six panda areas one from another, and the consequent vulnerability of the animals to the bamboo flowering, are all central to the efforts to conserve them.

Other inhabitants of the western highlands

In addition to the lesser panda, an unusual mixture of species share the giant panda's homeland. Some, like the giant panda itself, have been dis-

covered only in the last 150 years, and are still relatively unknown. Many are found only in this part of Asia. They include animals such as the pika, snow leopard and white-lipped deer from the cold north which love higher altitudes, and those such as the macaques, clouded leopard and serow which originated in warmer southern climes and prefer to frequent lower altitudes.

How can one help loving the charming creations of the hand of God, in the humblest of which the wisdom and admirable goodness of the Creator are manifested in a manner as marvellous, as astonishing, and as inconceivable in their way as the production and government of the infinite worlds that exist in space.

FROM THE DIARY OF PÈRE DAVID, 17 AUGUST, 1866, WHILE TRAVEL-LING IN MONGOLIA

The blue sheep, 'blue' because of its bluish-grey coat, lives in areas of rather stark and rocky terrain. (Ardea/Joanna Van Gruisen)

The giant panda rarely wanders into the treeless alpine regions where flocks of blue sheep roam. These agile animals prefer to keep close to the cliff edges so that they have a way of escape should a leopard appear. The blue sheep is in fact a sheep-like goat with a large head bearing cylindrical horns, and a bluish-grey coat that is paler on the underparts. Together with the goat-like tur of the Caucasus, it may well represent the only existing true link between the sheep and goat families.

The nocturnal snow leopard, the red fox and several hawks hunt in these regions, preying on small mammals such as pikas (mouse hares) and

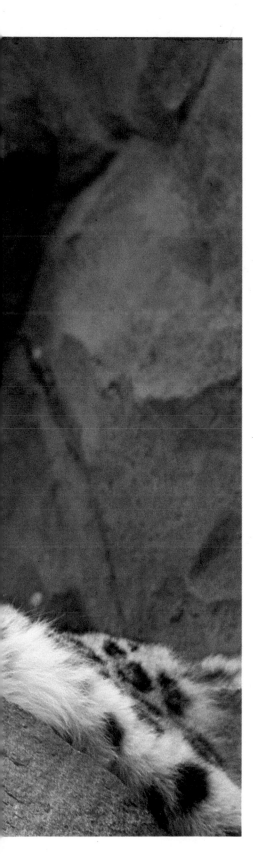

The beautiful snow leopard, which lives in the mountainous regions of Szechuan. (Ardea/ Kenneth W. Fink)

A male monal pheasant displaying its striking iridescent wing and head plumage. (Ardea/ Joanna Van Gruisen)

voles, and birds such as snow pigeons, rock bunting, ravens and larks. The snow leopard, its paw pads cushioned by a lush layer of fur to distribute is weight and insulate it against the cold, moves effortlessly across the snowfields and rocky screes to stalk bigger game such as wild goats and blue sheep. In winter most animals go down from the mountain summits, but a few, like the regal monal pheasant, stay there all year round.

The white-lipped or Thorold's deer, a lover of high places, is an endangered species confined to east and north Tibet and some adjoining mountainous areas of China, including Szechuan. Its coat is brown on the upper part of its body and creamy underneath, with a white nose, lips, chin and throat. Its numbers have been depleted by hunting to supply antlers for use in the preparation of traditional Oriental medicines.

In the high timber zone dominated by rhododendrons, the tragopan pheasant flaunts its iridescent plumage and, unlike other pheasants, elects to make its nest in trees. A wise precaution, for the dhole or red dog, a secretive, reddish-coloured canid that differs from all other dogs in having fewer molar teeth, hunts there. With the reputation of being a 'cruel' predator much given to disembowelling its victims, the red dog will gobble anything from deer and wild pigs to lizards, insects and berries.

The solitary serow moves silently through this part of the forest. It is a little-known, rather primitive goat-antelope about as big as a wild goat, though it is less agile and its legs are less well adapted for climbing. It is dark grey-brown in colour with long, tasselled ears, a long mane, short,

sharp horns and prominent glands close to the eyes that are used for scent-marking. At home on the timber-covered rock of upper forest, the serow is a plucky, aggressive individual, quick to defend its patch and food sources against interlopers of the same species. It has even been known to drive off attacking black bears successfully.

The Himalayan black bear of the Chinese forest is an omnivore who dines mainly on vegetation, with an occasional hors d'oeuvre of ants and grubs. Its Latin name means 'moon bear', and indeed the bear does sport a creamy crescent-moon mark on its black chest.

In the undergrowth beneath the rhododendron bushes scuttle a variety of mice and voles. Here, too, one can find the fascinating shrew mole, another 'link' animal that perhaps bridges the evolutionary gap between shrews and moles.

Within the main bamboo zone lives one of the shyest beasts in the western highlands, the takin or golden-fleeced cow. It is a large, rather bizarre relative of the musk ox, with a long shaggy coat and bulbous nose. In colour it is greyish-brown or, more spectacularly, golden with a dark stripe running along its back. A gregarious species and a nimble mountaineer, the takin is a distinctly smelly animal; the whole skin, rather than specialized glands, exudes a pungent odour and it has a burning taste. I assume

Temminck's tragopan, another unusual pheasant that shares the panda's terrain. Its stunning colouring makes it one of the most beautiful birds in the world. (Ardea/Kenneth W. Fink)

The dhole, or wild dog, poses a potential threat to young panda cubs, tending to hunt in packs numbering between 5 and 12. Dholes are hunted by man, their pelts sold at markets in the Szechuan region. (Ardea/Wardene Weisser)

A Szechuan takin, otherwise known as the golden-fleeced cow, normally lives in the more mountainous areas, feeding on grass, bamboo and tree shoots. It is sometimes in direct competition for food with the giant panda, and it is feared that where its predators have been removed in the wildlife reserves, their numbers may grow at an alarming rate, perhaps posing a further conservation problem. (Ardea/Kenneth W. Fink)

that hunters, who in the past valued the takin for its meat, found this out. Takins frequently spend the short summer on the high alpine meadows, grazing grass and herbage, but in the winter move down to crop bamboo and tree shoots. They prefer temperate conditions, steep land and plenty of tree cover at that time. Rarely seen in zoological collections, little is known about the ways of these creatures.

Monkeys such as the rare Père David's or Tibetan stump-tailed macaque and the striking golden monkey also live in the main bamboo zone. The latter have brown-gold coats with orange undersides, tail tip, legs and border round the face, a white muzzle, and bright blue around the nose and above the eyes. Primarily leaf-eaters, they also take fruit, pinecones, seeds, insects, birds and bird's eggs. Male golden monkeys resolutely defend their troupes, which may still number up to 500 or more on occasions, from predators such as the yellow-throated marten, another denizen of the bamboo thickets.

In the cold and wet season the golden monkeys, unlike the hardier macaques, migrate down to lower forest levels, and it is here that the most

The golden monkey, an extremely rare animal, has a thick coat of long, glossy bronze hair on its back and shoulders. (Ardea/Kenneth W. Fink)

The beautiful clouded leopard shares the panda's habitat; it is often the prey of hunters who prize its rare coat. (Ardea/Kenneth W. Fink)

glamorous of the tree-loving big cats, the clouded leopard, is found. It lives singly or, more rarely, in pairs up to an altitude of 2,500 m (8,200 ft). Heavily built with short legs and a long tail, this cat is a most accomplished climber – a veritable high-wire artiste – being able to swing along a branch hanging upside-down, descend a tree-trunk head first, and even dangle its body by a single hind-paw ready to drop onto a passing wild boar or deer. The Chinese call the clouded leopard the 'mint leopard' on account of the blotches on its coat, which resemble mint leaves in

shape. The clouded leopard also catches monkeys, squirrels and birds and likes to hunt at twilight, resting in a tree during the day and night.

And now there is but this track,
Steps cut here and there in stone,
Suspension bridges over raging torrents;
Crawling across, one catches a glimpse of the way
High up ahead, then looking down in terror finds below
The seething waters; not even the Yellow Crane could pass
Easily here; better for us to go on four feet like monkeys;
Around and then around that mountain of green clay we wind,
Nine twists to each hundred steps, panting for breath,
Each holding his chest with his hands,
Staggering towards the stars.

LI PAI, FROM *DOWN INTO SZECHUAN* (AD 701–762)

Another forest-dweller, the Asiatic golden cat or Temminck's cat, is also known in part of China as the rock cat or yellow leopard, and in Burma as the 'fire tiger'. Its combined head and body length is 75–105 cm (29^1/$_2$–41^1/$_2$ in), and it has a tail about 50 cm (19^3/$_4$ in) long. Its coat, though often a glorious golden red or golden brown, may also be dark brown or grey. Some are patterned with dark spots or stripes while others are unmarked. Usually a predator of birds and small mammals, the golden cat has been known to take deer, sheep, goats and water buffalo calves.

In the lower zone of the forests, the Himalayan crested porcupine, a nocturnal vegetarian, is frequently found sleeping by day in the sort of caves and hollow trees favoured by the pandas. When disturbed, these prickly creatures shake their quilled tails to produce a warning, rattling noise. They are regarded as pests by the peasants because of their habit of raiding crops.

These then are some of the giant panda's neighbours, co-habitants of its last refuge. None of them pose any threat to the survival of the panda population as a whole.

A wild boar, another inhabitant of the mountainous regions of Szechuan. Its snout is covered in snow as it has presumably been rooting for food. (Ardea/Stefan Meyers)

4

THE FOOD
OF THE
PANDA

But from the mountain's grassy side
A guiltless feast I bring;
A scrip with herbs and fruits supplied,
And water from the spring.

OLIVER GOLDSMITH, *THE VICAR OF WAKEFIELD* (CHAPTER 8)

A curious feature of this most curious of creatures is its almost total dependence for food on that unique and fascinating branch of the grasses, the bamboo.

Bamboo occurs throughout the tropics, and extends into sub-tropical and even temperate zones. It is even found as high as the snow-line in the Himalayas and the Andes. It has been used by man for millenia in an unusual variety of ways – as timber for house and boat building, split and stripped for weaving, for making weapons, cooking vessels, buckets, bottles and paper, and even, by virtue of its high content of gritty silica, as whetstones. It was in a hollow joint of bamboo that silk-worm eggs were carried from China to Byzantium during the reign of the Emperor Justinian. Young shoots can be eaten like asparagus; they can be salted, pickled or candied. Old plants secrete a fluid that is highly valued in traditional Oriental medicine, and bamboo has long been imported into the West to be fashioned into walking-sticks and basket-work.

Some species of these woody-stemmed plants can grow up to 36 m (118 ft) in height, at a rate of up to 40 cm (15³/₄ in) a day. Pandas select different parts of the bamboo plant, and sometimes different species (at least nine are acceptable to them), according to the time of year and the area that they are in. In some areas they are partial to varieties of *Sinarundinaria* – fung cane, chung China cane and fountain cane – while in others, species of *Phyllostachys*, or black cane, are their favourite. *Fargesia* is another popular type of bamboo. In spring, when most of the bamboo is low in protein as well as having unpalatable leaves, the animals prefer to crop the burgeoning new shoots, which are extra-rich in protein. In late summer

The giant panda will normally eat while in a sitting position, and takes its time over a meal, stripping and chewing the shoots and stems. (NHPA/ Philippa Scott)

Bamboo grows in thick clumps; pandas, with their thick coats, have little difficulty in penetrating the foliage to select juicy stems. (J. Knight)

and autumn, however, they concentrate on the leaves. The leaves of some types of bamboo die in winter, but the pandas still eat the dead foliage; other species retain their leaves all the year round.

The bamboo seeds, which are edible, and in some species are the size of pears, may on these occasions cover the ground to a depth of 12–15 cms. Throughout history, hungry peasants have gathered such sporadic bounty. Pandas, however, do not eat bamboo seed – and that is a great pity.

Any animal that eats indigestible plant material is faced with the problem of extracting nutrients from it. The leaves, shoots and branches of

plants contain the body-building protein and energy-giving fats and carbohydrates needed by the animals, but they are packed away inside cells whose walls are made of a tough and woody combination of cellulose and lignin.

Within the digestive systems of herbivores there are resident populations of bacteria able to break down cellulose by fermentation and thus crack open the cell walls. This releases the nutrients, which are then acted on by enzymes and absorbed into the blood and lymphatic systems through the intestinal wall.

Animals such as cattle and giraffes have a complex multiple-stomach arrangement. This includes the rumen, where some 1,000 billion bacteria act on the food. In horses and elephants, fermentation takes place in an enlarged caecum and colon further down the alimentary canal. To give more time for these processes to be carried out and for as much as possible of the products of digestion to be absorbed, all these herbivores also possess relatively long intestines.

The giant panda, on the other hand, takes on the fibrous, gritty bamboo without a specially adapted stomach, or bacteria to break it down, or a long intestinal tract. So how does it cope with its seemingly indigestible diet?

The short answer seems to be: not very efficiently. Although bamboo forms 99 per cent of the panda's diet, the animal is not endowed with special equipment to utilize it, and much of the nutritious content of the bamboo is not available to or digested by the panda. Pandas chew their food quickly, though not, except for the leaves, very well. The crudely chopped-up material is swallowed and acted upon by stomach acids and digestive enzymes in much the same way that a human alimentary canal works, and though there are some fermenting bacteria in its intestine, they almost certainly do very little. The panda absorbs only about 10 per cent of the food value in the bamboo, and this means that it has to eat a lot and process it through the body quickly to make room for more. The rapid passage of the bamboo along the animal's alimentary canal is aided by large quantities of lubricating mucus secreted by bowel walls that are unusually well supplied with mucus glands, and what goes in at one end of a panda looks very like what comes out at the other.

These pictures demonstrate the comparative sizes of two bamboo types – *Fargesia spatheca* (left) and *Sinarundinaria fangiana* (right) – and the appearance of after digestion by the giant panda. The amounts of indigestible woody cellulose and lignin are quite high, as shown by comparing the bulk of the plant both before and after cropping. (J. Knight)

It is possible that the panda also copes with its special diet by lowering its metabolic rate, as is done by sloths and koala bears, who also depend on a large volume/low yield diet of indigestible leaves. The panda's life-style, leisurely and undemanding, with little travelling and lots of sleep, reduces the demand for energy even further.

I worry about my pines and bamboos, both looking so dry and dead:
each day I am anxious about them, servants water their leaves
and irrigate their roots;
then a dark cloud rises
from the east and
a refreshing rain falls,
as refreshing as washing the dust from your
face or shampooing your hair; trees
flash their green twigs in welcome.

BAI JUYI, *THE GOOD RAIN* (C. AD 809)
Bai Juyi was a Tang Dynasty poet and, for 2 years, Governor of Shang Zian, Szechuan.

Bamboo has a potentially high food value with a protein content of about 15 per cent in the leaves (compared with 10–12 per cent in fresh meadow-grass), and 5 per cent in the shoots and stems. The soluble carbohydrate in all parts of the plant averages 12 per cent. Yet, to get the protein and energy it needs, a panda has to consume a large amount of bamboo every day. The actual amount cropped varies with the species of bamboo and the part of the plant taken in any particular season of the year. When dining on *Sinarundinaria* leaves and stems in summer, it eats about 12 kg (26½ lb), an amount that represents between 9 and 13 per cent of its bodyweight. During spring on a diet of *Fargesia* shoots they may scoff some 35 kg (77 lb). And where *Phyllostachys* shoots are the prime food item, pandas have been calculated to eat as much as 55 kg (120 lb), perhaps half their own body weight, in a day.

Because pandas eat a lot, they also defecate a lot – between 130 and 190 droppings each day – while feeding, walking or resting. With each dropping weighing about 150 g (5¼ oz), that can be as much as 28 kg (62 lb) of droppings produced in 24 hours.

It is puzzling that the giant panda depends for its survival on this tough plant with its hard stems and leaves charged with silica, the abrasive element that makes flint, quartz and sandstone what they are. After all, as we have seen, the panda is designed as a meat-eater, or at least as a meat-eater

This giant panda eats bamboo in a sedate
sitting position.
(J. Knight)

able to cope with an omnivorous diet. Why should it now spend so much of its time selecting and scrunching this fibrous and unappetizing plant? Having broken a tooth in half while foolishly trying to imitate a panda sitting beside me munching bamboo, it is a subject close to my heart.

The explanation must lie in the fact that in its homeland there is nothing else that can provide a sufficient, year-round source of food.

Though bamboo is almost the only food that giant pandas eat, they do from time to time feed on other items, of both a vegetable and an animal nature. Over thirty different occasional foods have been recorded, including tree bark, horse-tails, water-weed, vines, wild parsnips and fungi. More rarely perhaps, for it is not a natural predator, the giant panda has the good fortune to come across an animal that it can catch and eat; or more likely, finds a dead or dying individual. Analyses of panda droppings have revealed the remains of such creatures as mice, rats, deer and even monkeys.

The lesser panda's appetite is somewhat more catholic than that of the giant panda. As well as eating bamboo shoots, it will take grasses, herbs, fruits, nuts, roots, lichens, small mammals, bird's eggs, insects and grubs, hunting for some of these on the ground at night.

Given the opportunity, giant pandas will happily switch to other foods, proving themselves in the process to be omnivores at heart. In zoos they quickly come to relish fruits, vegetables, cereals, pulses, eggs and cooked meat, and their appetite for bamboo often drops sharply. The zoo pandas under my care dine enthusiastically on apples and a porridge containing boiled rice, yoghurt and a type of 'complete' invalid diet powder. Sometimes they show little interest in bamboo and even when they do, seldom eat more than 5 or 6 kg (11-13$^{1}/_{4}$ lb) a day.

People living near giant panda country say that the animals are particularly fond of cooked pork and will go so far as to raid wood-cutters' huts in order to steal such food if they catch a whiff of cooking on the breeze. There is a story about a female panda who, in January 1985, broke into a tent in one of the wildlife monitoring stations set up in the Wolong Nature Reserve, Szechuan. It scoffed two cooked legs of mutton and a quantity of sugar-cane and then drank a couple of tubs of sugar water proffered by members of the staff. Having dined well, the animal pawed quilts and sleeping bags down onto the ground, made itself comfortable on them and went to sleep. Next morning, hungry once more, it sat on and crushed a cooking stove while trying to reach some bacon hanging on a tent-pole. This panda was to become a regular visitor to the camp, forever cadging food.

Other creatures – deer, wild pigs, bears, porcupines, monkeys and insects – feed, with varying degrees of frequency, on the bamboo, but apart perhaps from certain flies and beetles, none is so fundamentally dependent upon the plant. The panda, like the sloths in South America (which possess an advantage over the panda – a large, multi-compartmental stomach full of cellulose-digesting bacteria), found an ecological niche for itself, one with a food supply that wasn't exploited significantly by any other medium- or large-sized animal. It became a specialist among specialists, and there was no harm in that, for the bamboo forests of China

once covered enormous areas. The panda wasn't physically well-equipped to digest it, but the plant was so plentiful that it could afford to be inefficient at processing it.

As the millenia slipped by the panda grew larger: energy conservation is more efficient in bigger bodies, and they retain the heat more easily in cold, damp conditions. The seasonal selectivity of the animal's feeding habits and its way of browsing, tending to prefer plants on the edges of bamboo clumps and taking shoots, stems or leaves of only certain sizes, did not have any adverse effect on the overall population of bamboo.

Pandas can be quite lively at times; here a giant panda can be seen gnawing on a piece of wood. (Rex Features/Peter Brooker)

A giant panda searches for food in the kitchen of a Chinese home. Pandas can adapt fairly quickly to foodstuffs other than bamboo and there are several accounts of pandas raiding peasants' kitchens and food supplies. (Rex Features)

Pandas and bamboo lived happily together and the animals' fussy cropping represented a sort of effective horticulture; by eating, for example, shoots of a particular size at certain times and in certain locations, the pandas influenced the density and spread of bamboo clumps.

The bamboo flowering

A remarkable and little understood feature of the bamboo is the way in which it flowers. There are long intervals between flowerings. In some species, such as *Phyllostachys bambusoides*, this can be as much as 120 years. The two species more commonly cropped by the pandas, *Fargesia* and *Sinarundinaria*, have flowering intervals of about 70 to 80 years and 42 to 48 years respectively. The flowering is significant to the pandas, and potentially tragic, because it is quickly followed by the seeding and dying back of the plant.

The Chinese have been intrigued by and have recorded the snail's pace life-cycle of bamboo for centuries, even though few human beings live to witness more than one flowering of a particular species such as *Phyllostachys*. Their archives contain accounts of *Phyllostachys* flowering in the years AD 919 and 1114, in the 1720s and the 1840s; the 120-year cycle stretches back into the mists of time. Another species of *Phyllostachys*

which was taken to Japan from China over 1000 years ago is known to have flowered in 813, 931, 1247, 1666, 1768, 1848, 1908 and 1968 – it has a cycle of approximately 60 years. To date, no one has discovered where the mechanism is that counts off the decades with such surprising accuracy.

Sometimes just a clump or stand of one species flowers; at other times several bamboo species, covering perhaps the slopes of a whole range of mountains, all burst into bloom together. Occasionally, one species will flower at one and the same time all over the world. In the late 1960s *Phyllostachys* flowered simultaneously in China, Japan, the USA, Britain and Russia. The bamboo flowering is followed by the dying back of the plant, thereby letting in much needed sunlight for the new seedlings. In times past, pandas affected by a die-back simply moved on to places where the bamboo had not flowered; starvation was most unlikely.

Today, the situation has changed; the panda's extreme specialization combines with the flowering phenomenon to threaten its very existence. During the twentieth century the bamboo forests have not only grown smaller, but, more ominously, they have become fragmented. Now, when the bamboo flowers, a panda cannot amble off to pastures new because there is no adjoining, non-flowering bamboo zone. With no adequate alternative food source to fall back on, the pandas die of famine.

The flower of the bamboo plant (identified here by its white markings on a deep purple background) is not particularly beautiful or ornate but its appearance heralds a general dying back of the bamboo plant as a whole, as shown in the right-hand picture. (J. Knight)

5

THE LIFE
IN A DAY OF
THE PANDA

About the woodlands I will go,
To see the cherry hung with snow.
A.E. HOUSEMAN, *A SHROPSHIRE LAD*

Man-Man, which translates as 'slowly'.

To share a day in the life of a typical giant panda, in the light of what we presently know about the animal's habits, let us take an imaginary adult male, and spy on him. I shall call him Man-Man, which in Chinese means 'slowly'. Such appellation seems appropriate to his personality, for he is a quiet plodder, apparently content in his sub-alpine fastnesses of tree-girt mountainsides, bounding brooks and mist-veiled air. He leads a hum-drum life, half rest, half food-gathering, with seldom any alarm to break his peaceful solitude where the only sounds are those of water-splash, bird-song and breeze-stirred leaves. Man-Man's days, we might well suppose, are halcyon ones.

Man-Man is eight years old and, like other male pandas, is laird of a patch of land that to him is home. Only about 6 square km (2¼ sq miles) in size, it is slightly bigger than that of a female giant panda, and overlaps with those of three females and an equal number of males. Most of it covers an area of the upper slopes where tall dragon spruce and Faber fur forest, often 50 m (65 ft) high, forms a canopy above vast stands of fountain bamboo (*Sinarundinaria nitida*). The terrain is more sloping than would have been selected by a female panda for her home range, but needs must, and the key feature of a male's stamping ground is the proximity of some female ranges at mating time.

Man-Man spends a considerable amount of his time wandering outside his territory, checking on the other pandas in his neighbourhood, not so much keeping an eye on them, more a nose and an ear. This isn't to say he is in any way proprietorial about his plot of land – not a bit of it. Pandas' home ranges overlap, and while females will discourage other females and sub-adults from trespassing on their core areas, the really homely 5 per cent to 8 per cent of their ranges where they spend the major amount of their time, males have less well developed core areas, don't worry about

Man-Man begins the day with a quick meal of bamboo leaves. (Bruce Coleman/WWF/Kojo Tanaka)

Up a tree to see what the day holds. (Bruce Coleman/WWF/Kojo Tanaka)

other males travelling through, and don't patrol or mark borders in the manner of many carnivores. While hardly putting out the 'welcome' mat, giant pandas certainly do not reach for the shotgun nor stick up 'trespassers will be prosecuted' signs. Even the core areas of female ranges may overlap. The core areas are generally above an altitude of 2,700 m (8,860 ft) and, as in the case of most of Man-Man's range, face south or west – the snow doesn't lie so long here. Man-Man particularly favours this sort of place because the high tree canopy encourages a lusher and more open growth of bamboo below it. Where there is no tree cover, the bamboo is denser and dryer. For the same reason, pandas rarely settle in areas logged by man, as tree-felling leads to tight-packed growth of poor quality bamboo, particularly fountain bamboo, with thin and unappetizing stems. Besides, as Man-Man dimly realizes, trees afford hollow trunks that neighbouring females can turn into good dry dens, ideal for cubbing.

Man-Man gets to his feet and moves off for another stroll. (Bruce Coleman/WWF/ Kojo Tanaka)

Like most males Man-Man rarely visits some parts of his range – much depends on the food supply, and indeed, as I have just said, he spends a lot of the year, particularly between November and June, on walkabout. In summer he seldom roams, and is usually to be found 'at home'. Why, you might ask, do pandas have such small territories when other animals, like tigers, are known to have home ranges from 50 to 10,000 sq km (19–3,860 sq miles) in size? The answer is food supply. The tiger hunts over a smaller stretch of land where game is plentiful and over a much vaster area when there are no easy pickings; the panda is surrounded by a plentiful food source for which it has little competition and which doesn't tend to run away.

As we join Man-Man, it is daybreak on a September morning. The sky is the colour of a dolphin's back, black clouds obscure the mountain tops and a milky mist has dropped like a still and shredded curtain around the crowns of the conifer trees. It will rain again soon for the monsoon is still

(left) The encroachment of agriculture upon the areas inhabited by the panda; here the crops indicate how far the ploughed and planted fields and terraces have moved into what was once uncultivated land. (J. Knight)

(right) Much of the terrain Man-Man moves in is misty and damp at least for part of the day; these conditions do not trouble him as his coat is thick and adapted to such weather. (J. Knight)

here. Man-Man, snug in his greasy, tight-packed coat of hair, is resting in the middle of a clump of bamboo, his back against a long fallen log encrusted with moss and fungus – one of his regular napping spots. He yawns and briefly displays yellow fangs and a healthy pink tongue. Should it, as seems certain, start to pour with rain for the rest of the day, there is a spruce tree a few paces away with a hollow trunk, the cavity conveniently panda-sized. Man-Man doesn't mind winter cold or the drizzly rain of spring, but he is not too keen when the summer monsoon buckets down; then he seeks shelter. Pandas, by and large, are weatherproof, but

avoid heavy, long-lasting downpours whenever possible. During the night Man–Man did a bit of foraging for bamboo leaves – easy to eat and especially nutritious in autumn. Pandas go about their business at any time of the day or night but are most active at twilight, dawn or dusk. In spring, when the animals feed on bamboo stems of lower nutritional value and shoots which are higher in water content and need peeling, they have to spend more time feeding and, as a consequence, are then busier than in summer and autumn when leaves are the principal food source. In winter they are more active at night than in the other seasons.

Deep within the woods, Man-Man sits back and eats once more. (Bruce Coleman/WWF/ Timm Rautert)

But to see Man-Man and his sort at their busiest, one should go looking for them at dusk on an April evening when the new *Fargesia* shoots have sprouted.

Our panda scratches his ample belly with a hind foot and rolls forward into a standing position. Time to go feeding again. Though pandas rest for almost ten hours out of twenty-four, the rest of the time is largely spent eating. Being such inefficient digesters and needing to swallow such a large volume of bamboo, they have to work at their food gathering.

As Man-Man moves on into the bamboo thicket, he pauses to sniff at and then chomp, a small bunch of blackberries and in so doing disturbs a fat tragopan pheasant that bustles off under a rhododendron bush. Ambling slowly along a familiar soggy trail – pandas generally walk at no more than 3–5 km (2–3 miles) an hour – Man-Man defecates and urinates as he goes. Every now and then he stops to crop a posy of leaves from the ranks of tall bamboo plants on either side. He ignores the apricot, cream and bright yellow autumn mushrooms poking up through the under-growth and clinging to the damp bark of Chinese pine and Hemlock spruce, and the rock squirrels feverishly dashing hither and thither to feed on the nuts of occasional hazel trees in preparation for winter hibernation. Pandas don't hibernate like bears, don't gather stores of provisions against the winter days like non-hibernating tree squirrels, don't even put on extra layers of fat as a food reserve and insulation for the cold and snowy weather. They just keep on eating – all year round.

> *Few guests come to my home*
> *while below the terrace are*
> *many bamboos and pines; under*
> *the shade of the western wall*
> *autumn colours linger*
> *and a chilly wind blows*
> *through the eastern room;*
> *I have a flute but I am too lazy*
> *to play it; I have many books, but*
> *they all go unread; I live through each day*
> *with no particular desires or worries;*
> *who needs a large house to live in? isn't it*
> *useless to store up grain?*
>
> BAI JUYI, *AT HOME ON AN AUTUMN DAY*

As predicted it starts to rain steadily, though it is lighter now and the sky has turned to dove grey. Man-Man doesn't seem to notice the rain. He reaches a more open place where the bamboo growth is broken by low mountain ashes dotted about. One of these trees is a regular marking post of his. Turning his back to it he rubs his bottom against the tree bark and then climbs *backwards* up the trunk into a most curious position – he looks

An unusual sighting of the giant panda out in an open clearing. (J. Knight)

almost as if he's doing a handstand against the mountain ash. Wagging his apology for a tail, but one that nevertheless makes a useful paintbrush, he thoroughly wipes some of his anal sac secretions on to the blackened bark. A trio of small and dumpy flowerpeckers visiting a Japanese honeysuckle trailing up a nearby tree briefly interrupt their nectar-gathering to regard the panda perform his scent-making ritual. Man–Man pushes himself away from the mountain ash and there is a soft plop as his hind feet land again on the ground. He turns, briefly sniffs his scent mark, and then with heavy rolling gait, goes back to his trail and enters the palisade of bamboo once more.

A few metres in he stops and squats on his buttocks – the bamboo leaves are in prime condition and bejewelled with raindrops. They crown his head like a wreath of laurels. Comfortably seated, he reaches up with his right fore-paw and, grasping a thick stem of bamboo with his dextrous claws, bends it down, sniffs it, looks at it closely, and then moves it towards his mouth. Holding it at right angles to his jaws, he quickly snips off a length of stem with his cheek teeth and munches the leaves while reaching slowly for another cane.

Pandas are very selective in the kind of bamboo and the parts of a plant they will eat. I have already mentioned how leaves are mainly eaten at one

time of year and stems or new shoots at others. The size and length of shoots and stems is also important. Man-Man and his kith and kin go for longer, thicker shoots, the ones that grow on the periphery of the bamboo stands. Sometimes pandas first gather a fistful of leaves before lying back to enjoy them one at a time, picking each out of the mouth and holding it neatly in the paw to be munched. When dealing with the thicker stems, they will frequently strip off the tough outer layers with their teeth before chewing.

Man-Man is off again. He walks slowly out of the bamboo and turns downhill. Crossing a grassy area, he makes for a large rhododendron bush the centre of which forms a dry and tent-like hollow. A pair of blood pheasants stalk out as he enters. He sniffs at a stained and crooked root that juts out of the soil. There is the acidic smell of another male's scent mark. Only Man-Man can interpret the message it bears. He goes over to a small pile of old droppings and sniffs again. Same male.

Man-Man goes out into the rain again. He's in one of his fussy feeding moods. Some days he feeds intensively on just one or two stands of bamboo, moving steadily around the edges. On others, like now, he nibbles a bit here, a bit there, and keeps moving on from stand to stand. Negotiating a steep terrace of rock with crevices filled with fading yellow balsam whose seed-vessels burst wherever a broad black paw brushes them, he reaches a wide ledge that supports a copse of dripping Armand pines rising above a shrub layer of black bamboo and viburnum. Our panda stops to feed again. He's now in a part of his range which overlaps that of an old and particularly short-tempered female. He scent marks the trunk of a pine, passing a little urine as he does so, and scratches the bark with his sharp fore claws several times before beginning to eat. Pandas prefer to use conifers as scent posts. As well as scent marking with or without a dribble of urine, clawing and biting trees and sometimes stripping off bark, pandas also rub and roll on the ground and rake it with their claws. The purpose of all this seems to be communication: to leave signs, visual or olfactory, for other pandas, and most probably the signs contain encoded information that we humans can never hope to decipher. Cats and other carnivores use a similar system, but where they employ it, among other reasons, to stake out the boundaries of their territory, pandas do not. After all, they are not, like tigers or city tom cats, jealous of their property, and though some trees are regularly scent marked, these are situated on well-travelled trails, *not* on range borders.

So what might the smelly and scratchy signals convey? We can only guess that they speak of gender, age, family tree, status in the panda hierarchy and sexual matters – but *maybe* there's panda gossip in there somewhere too! Female pandas leave marks much less frequently than males except during their oestrus periods, so in panda society it seems it's the males who do all the 'talking'.

Man-Man sits down in a favourite place, back against an old cherry tree. During the spring he often comes here to crop the new shoots which are then growing at a rate of over 15 cm (6 in) a day. At those times, with the sun shining and flowers blooming in the open meadows and along his pathways, he takes a length of bamboo cane between his paws and strips

Man-Man negotiates a steep terrace of rock covered in the colourful-leaved shrubs which flourish on the mountainside. (Rex Features)

off the hairy outer sheaths of the shoots by nipping them with his cheek or front teeth and pulling back his head. A litter of discarded sheaths lie around him. In fact they make this spot even more comfortable to sit in while the May cherry blossoms fall around him.

Now the rain is slackening and a silver-coloured break in the clouds appears above the mountain peaks. Man-Man looks up, his impassive Pierrot face glinting with moisture. No shoots around now, but the leaves

are tasty. Feeling, as ever, quintessentially laid back – which indeed he is in more ways than one – the panda bites through a tall cane to bring its leaves falling on to his head. Chomping them steadily he's already selecting his next morsel. With his right paw he reaches for an even thicker heavily leafed cane and bends it down to him in an arch. Then he traps it with both hind paws while he pushes stems and leaves, one at a time, into the side of his mouth. When all the choicest bits of the plant have been consumed, he

Man-Man pauses to sniff at the trunk of a tree to assess the proximity of other pandas which may have left a scent mark on the bark. (Bruce Coleman/WWF/Timm Rautert)

releases the cane and it whips erect with a whirr that startles a small flock of babblers into the air.

Man-Man combs the back of his right ear with the nails of his right fore-paw and stares blankly up at the grey sky. Something moves in the corner of his eye. He looks down at a small brown creature with eyes like wet blackcurrants watching him from the hole beneath a bamboo root. It is a bamboo rat – a rodent that is almost as fond of bamboo as Man-Man himself. Unexpectedly Man-Man swats at it with a paw, but he's too slow – he usually is. On the odd occasion, he has managed to grab a rat less alert than this one, and after killing and playing with it rather like a cat with a mouse, eaten it. No matter, the panda is utterly unconcerned about the rat's escape. He doesn't start sniffing and scratching at the hole in the frustrated manner of the fox or marten. Time for a rest.

Man-Man gets to his feet again and shuffles off through the bamboo. Pandas don't have lairs or dens, except when the female is raising young. They rest or sleep where they happen to be, curling up quite happily even in the snow – but they do know the most comfortable places and these they will visit time and again. As they rest for almost ten hours out of every day, made up of periods that may last as long as six hours or more, or no more than a few minutes when in one of their restless moods, the snugness of their resting-places is a matter of some importance to them. A 'good' place has something to sit or lie against – it can be a rock, a fallen log or a hollow tree. Bamboos should be within easy, preferably arm's reach where the accumulated bits of discarded plant material serve as fine bedding. I am sure that pandas deserve their comfortable, contemplative, untroubled rests, for during the remainder of the day and night they live to eat and eat to live. There is little time in a panda's life for anything else. Perhaps that's the reason for their solitary existence – socializing would waste too many hours on communicating, quarrelling, competing and courting with one's fellows, hours that are needed for the provisioning of that curious digestive system. Better to be a hermit. Perhaps the real fun of being a panda is just the sitting and thinking on a full stomach.

Man-Man has only to walk about 15 m (50 ft) to find one of his best rest-places. It is the dead stump of a dragon spruce on the edge of the pine copse, where the ledge ends in a near vertical cliff that falls down into a deep and narrow gorge. Here the panda can sprawl, belly up, and by turning his head, see with one eye the thin white worm that is the river of rushing water far below. The spread of pine above him keeps off most of the rain. This morning, as black crows rise out of the gorge on up-draughts of mild, rain-laced air, Man-Man elects to sleep for a while and snuggles up against his stump.

Not having a permanent lair, wandering about the mountains cropping bamboo without fear of trespassing on other pandas' property, Man-Man and his ilk might be expected to clock up a fair number of kilometres during their travels. Not so. Pandas don't usually move fast – Man-Man is not christened 'Slowly' without reason – and though they can go as far as 4 km in a day on their meanderings, a $\frac{1}{2}$ km (a mere $\frac{1}{4}$ mile), is the more usual average.

Light cloud and a soft wind
that blows over the flowers
and through willows at noon
as I cross the stream;
others do not understand
what is in my heart; thinking
of me too simply
as a pleasure-loving lad.

CHENG HAO, *SPRING INTERLUDE* (AD 1032–1085)

Moving off through the undergrowth again, Man-Man searches for a comfortable resting place or clump of bamboo. (Bruce Coleman/WWF/Timm Rautert)

It is noon and the sky is an up-turned pewter bowl. The rain descends unremittingly. With a great stretch of his limbs, Man-Man awakes, scratches his chest vigorously, and pulls himself up into a sitting position.

Reclining on a large stump, Man-Man takes stock of the land. (Bruce Coleman/WWF/Kojo Tanaka)

The habitat in which Man-Man roams has several fast-moving mountain streams which irrigate the vegetation on the banks and provide drinking water for the animals. (J. Knight)

He looks around. Mist fills the gorge and there is no sound but the soft dripping of water. While his outer coat is wet, his dense undercoat is dry, and he feels fine. Even in the winter snows, Man–Man is well protected against the cold.

The panda pulls a few bamboo stems towards him and neatly bites off their upper extremities. Licking lips fringed with grey hairs, he stands up and ambles away. Time for a drink. Turning his back on the cliff edge, he follows a narrow trail roofed with arching bamboo that leads steeply downhill towards a ridge covered with open dry brush. There, in a hollow, lies a bubbling pool whose source is a thick cascade of water emerging from a low pile of mossy rock. Man-Man goes to the pool edge and lowers his head to the reeds to suck up water. Pandas live in a damp environment and often, as today, the bamboo is sopping wet, but their droppings contain more water than the food they eat, except when feeding on the shoots in spring. Man-Man drinks at one of the many mountain streams and pools that he knows once or twice a day. During the winter when thick ice covers the water, he goes down to the valley where the streams still run freely. Once in a while Man-Man for some reason has a water binge and drinks an unusually large amount in one go. Then he lies for some time, his paunch bloated like Falstaff's, beside the water's edge.

After tasting the cold clear water of the pool, Man-Man sets off uphill at a very slow plod, stripping bamboo leaves every now and then. The gradient soon gets steeper and the going harder. Maybe this tough, though spectacular, terrain is the reason why male pandas, in particular, don't travel very far and thereby miss out on more mating opportunities. Or are they, perish the thought, just a little lazy?

Man-Man is now heading for the highest part of his range, a patch of spruce forest underlaid by beds of pure Fang cane, at an altitude of over 3,000 m (9,845 ft). Sometimes, even in the winter, he spends several days at a time up here, and in the short season of spring sunshine he occasionally climbs up into the fork of a tree that is also one of his regular scent posts, and warms his belly in the golden rays. Pandas are moderately good climbers, but despite claims made to the contrary, don't go in for climbing much. When they do, apart from the odd spot of sun-worshipping, it is usually to escape marauding red dogs, men or other male pandas.

Man-Man's sensitive nose picks up a strange scent in the wet air. He stops and looks in the direction from which it is drifting. Leopard! And there it is, a golden cash leopard, a rare visitor to his range, lying on a low spruce branch and staring at him, long tail twitching. Man-Man stares straight back, giving the leopard a good view of his distinctive warning patterning by slightly lowering his head so that his black ears are framed against white shoulders. 'Don't even think of it!' is the message implied. The leopard does think of it, but swiftly abandons the idea. Man-Man is an adult panda and, the cat instinctively knows, a doughty fighter if put to it. Leopards do take a small number of young pandas – how many we don't know – but their main prey in these parts is deer, particularly tufted deer. Studies of leopard droppings have revealed panda remains in a little over $^1/_2$ per cent of them, while evidence of deer eating was present in almost 90 per cent. Pandas like Man-Man might be harassed on rare occasions by red dogs or black bears, but on the whole enemies are very few and far between. Opening his mouth, Man-Man briefly utters a short throaty huffing sound – an apprehensive threat – and moves on through the bamboo. Eyes bright, the leopard watches him disappear and does nothing.

The panda, munching as he goes, makes for a rhododendron bush. It's raining very heavily now, and he will shelter there, dozing peacefully for most of the early afternoon.

By four o'clock Man-Man's stomach rumblings bring him out of his slumbers. Oh, for a bouquet of rain-washed bamboo leaves! Blinking, he

peers through the rhododendron foliage and, spying a likely cane, grasps it firmly and pulls it, creaking, into his shelter. He sets about assuaging his hunger pangs by briskly stripping the plant. A few minutes later he sets out into the rain with the idea of visiting a part of the forest nearby that not only, to his mind, supports some of the most toothsome autumn bamboo in the Middle Kingdom, but is also where his domain mingles with that of a female panda, an animal which he's only ever seen twice, and then very

A chance encounter with a leopard passes off smoothly – normally the panda and the leopard live side by side without strife. (Survival Anglia/Dieter & Mary Plage)

briefly, at mating time, last year and the year before that. He has no intention, however, of now seeking out the female. Pandas are not at all sociable outside the short mating season, in fact they are positively unclubbable. Their nature is to be, as Dickens wrote in *A Christmas Carol* in another context, 'secret and self-contained, and solitary as an oyster'.

Man–Man sniffs and listens as he walks through the forest, but utters no sound. Not that he can't vocalize; pandas are capable of producing a range of at least eleven sounds, from the huffing our friend delivered in front of the leopard, through snorts, honks, moans, bleats, squeals and chirps to growls and roars. While honks and squeals are usually associated with apprehension and distress, growls are threats and chirps seem to be for chit-chatting between individuals. Most vocalization occurs during courtship or the occasional confrontations. And sometimes a series of different sounds at varying volumes may be emitted to form a 'string of words' that can convey emotions, attitudes and intentions. When I am called upon to inject a giant panda restrained in the treatment room, it will usually perform the most agile acrobatics in trying to avoid the approaching needle, but very rarely am I cursed with a bark or a roar, or indeed any sound at all. Where lions roar and wolves howl to notify all concerned of their presence, pandas generally go silently about their daily business.

Man-Man finds himself on the bank of a shallow, fast-running stream that winds through the trees. He sniffs the water, decides not to drink and promptly wades across. If it had been any deeper he would have swum across without any trouble, using a sturdy dog-paddle. On dry land again, he eats bamboo for a few minutes and immediately afterwards approaches a tree with the intention of scratching it. Then it happens! A black-and-white face peeps out from behind the tree trunk. The female. At first both pandas stand stock still. Presently the female moves away from the tree and shows herself fully. She obviously doesn't like what she sees and gives a couple of short snorts. Facing her, ten paces away, Man-Man isn't very impressed either. She growls and stares intently at him. To show he is not aggressive, Man-Man first turns his head away, and then lifts his left paw to cover the mask of his face. The female snorts again. Man-Man thereupon dramatically reinforces his pacific signals by sticking his head between his fore-legs. The female gives a short huff and walks away into the cover of the bamboo without looking back.

Meetings of pandas, infrequent outside the mating season of March through May, are usually like that. Body postures and vocalizations get the anti-pathetic messages across. As with the leopard Man-Man displayed his markings to full effect when in aggressive mood, so he plays them down when anxious to placate. Whatever the emotion in any given situation, however, the panda's facial expression never changes. His is the inscrutable oriental mask, with none of the signals contained within the grimaces of the canine and feline tribes. Vocalization may be pronounced during encounters, and can continue for an hour or two. A pair of pandas may even play and there is rarely any fighting. If pandas do engage in battle, it is in the manner of bears, with much clawing, gnawing and roaring, but rarely any blood spilt. During most of the year, chance meetings end quickly with each party going his or her own way.

Dusk is approaching. Man-Man finds a tall stand of bamboo with an extra treat of some juicy sugar-cane growing at its edge that will make a fine dessert. The day, with its brushes with the leopard and the female panda, has been an unusual and exciting one for our subject. As the light fades and the last of the red and yellow sunbirds leave the forest to fly south for the winter, Man-Man, impassive as ever, looks forward to a quiet night of sleeping and feeding, sleeping and feeding, sleeping and feeding.

Man-Man searches for a comfortable resting place for the night. Giant pandas normally only sleep in dens when they have young to protect and care for; otherwise they sleep in the open on a bed of moss or leaves. (Bruce Coleman/WWF/Timm Rautert)

By the side of the Hao river, Zhuangzi★
had a useless argument
with Huizi★ about whether a person
could really understand what animals feel; an
otter tried to catch a fish;
the fish leaped up, not because
it was happy, but because it was
being chased!

BAI JUYI, *BY THE SIDE OF A POND* (AD 842)

★Famous Taoist philosophers of the Zhou Dynasty who argued over whether animals could experience joy.

6

REPRODUCTION
IN THE
GIANT PANDA

The female overcomes the male with stillness,
Lying low in stillness.

LAO TSE, *TAO-TE-CHING* (604–C.531 BC)

I love the Baby Giant Panda,
I'd welcome one to my veranda.

OGDEN NASH, *THE PANDA*

Apart from the occasional chance encounters, which are not normally marked by demonstrations of good fellowship, and the very rare gatherings of up to fourteen pandas which have been recorded when the bamboo has flowered and hungry animals congregate around the available food, the social life of the giant panda revolves around the annual mating season, which usually runs from the middle of March to the middle of May with maximum activity in April. Though the female generally comes into oestrus ('heat' or 'season') but once a year, it is possible that, in some cases, there is a second, weaker oestrus period in autumn.

During the mating season the male pandas's testes increase in size. Up to puberty at the age of $5^1/_2$ to $6^1/_2$ years, the testes are buried in the fatty subcutaneous tissue of the groin, and are difficult to locate. Indeed, Desmond Morris in his book *Men and Pandas*, published almost a quarter of a century ago, stated that the male sex organs were normally hidden and lacked a scrotum. In fact, sexually mature male pandas do possess a scrotum and easily discernible, well-descended testes; the explanation for Morris's statement is that all of the male pandas closely examined by zoologists up to the mid 1960s were young ones, in whom sexing can, at first sight, be difficult.

The female's oestrus period lasts for two to three weeks. During the first part of the period, before ovulation, her behaviour pattern alters. She becomes restless and more vocal, her appetite decreases and she scent-marks more frequently. The scent and the vocalization attract the attention of males in the vicinity, who come urgently to court the female. The

The result of a successful panda pregnancy – today zoos play an important part in boosting the birth rate of panda cubs. (J.M. Martos)

A female giant panda scent-marks the ground as she comes into oestrus (J. Knight)

males, also anxious to advertise their presence and intent, become more active and vocal during this time. They will moan, bleat, chirp and growl, sometimes from a perch up in a tree, and loudly enough to be heard a couple of kilometres (about one mile) away.

During this time, physical encounters between pandas occur more frequently, females often initiating teasing, introductory wrestling and biting contests, and males fighting like clumsy wrestlers for the favours of a particular female. The female will permit the male to mount her during only two or three days of the oestrus period, around the time of ovulation. She becomes more amenable, even mildly flirtatious, presenting her rump to her mate and sometimes backing up towards him, whereupon the male takes the initiative, copulating several times, though only briefly, while standing or squatting behind her with his forepaws on her back. When mounted, the male does occasionally bite the female's neck in a manner similar to that of the cat. Copulation in the giant panda lasts between 30 seconds and 5 minutes, rather less than the time recorded in carnivores such as the brown bear (up to 2 hours) and the ferret (up to 3 hours). The female rejects her partner after copulation by snapping at him or running off.

Up to five or six males may assemble in the hope of mating a female, and will squabble among themselves while waiting for her to ovulate. If

The pandas' courtship behaviour often includes wrestling foreplay. (J. Knight)

she moves off, they follow – full of hope. In the panda hierarchy of a particular area of forest one male will be the dominant individual. Although he usually exercises *droit de seigneur* and mates first with a female, he does not stay and guard her after the coupling as is the case with some other carnivores. She may subsequently be mated by other males but this does not seem to trouble the boss panda.

Whereas in cats the little bone within the penis, and the spines on its exterior surface, trigger ovulation at the moment of penetration by stimulating a nervous reflex, such induced ovulation is not thought to occur in the panda, even though it too has some bone in its rather small penis. Ovulation is almost certainly a spontaneous occurrence.

Pregnancy in the giant panda lasts between 3 and 5^1/$_2$ months, the reason for this variance being the phenomenon, which occurs in some mammals, called delayed implantation. After fertilization, the egg of the panda divides repeatedly in the usual manner until it reaches the blastocyst stage, at which point it is in the form of a microscopic hollow ball of about 128 cells. In other species – humans, dogs, or elephants, for example – the blastocyst then implants itself in the lining of the uterus and continues to develop. In species where delayed implantation occurs, the blastocyst floats around idly for a variable length of time in the interior of the uterus

At times, during oestrus, the female panda will act provocatively, presenting her hindquarters to the male. (J. Knight)

before implanting and continuing with its development. In many cases, this hiatus in embryonic growth serves the useful purpose of allowing the young to be born at times of year most favourable to both neo-nate and mother: when there is good weather or an abundance of food, for example. We do not fully understand how the delay is controlled but it is certainly a hormonal mechanism and may involve the length of daylight as perceived subconsciously by the eyes. In giant pandas the implantation delay seems to vary between $1^1/_2$ and 4 months.

The female will find a den, such as a hollow tree trunk or dry cave, in which to give birth, and may do a little nest-making with pieces of bark and bamboo. Although pandas normally defecate wherever they happen to be, while walking, eating or resting, females keep their breeding dens clean. Once the cubs are born, she will frequently block the den with her own body to protect the cubs and, most importantly, to keep the temperature and humidity from dropping too low.

Pandas give birth to one or two (rarely three) cubs, and will usually attempt to raise only one, generally the larger, of a pair of twins. The birth process is normally quick and undramatic. The baby emerges without much fuss or heavy bearing-down on the part of the mother, followed within half an hour by the next where twins are present. The cub's wrig-

Copulation takes place. (J. Knight)

gling and squealing immediately attracts the mother's attention, and she will pick it up neatly and gently using her bamboo-grasping thumb, and begin to nurse it.

Because of the relatively lengthy delay in implantation, the baby panda is born looking remarkably small for one gestated so long. A newborn panda is about the same size and shape as a newborn Labrador puppy. It weighs between 100 and 150 g ($3^1/2$ to $5^1/4$ oz), measures around 16 cm ($6^1/2$ in) in length and is almost naked, covered only by a sparse layer of white hair totally lacking any black markings. It is born blind and helpless, and possesses much more of a tail than the adult.

For the first 3 weeks the mother will seldom put the cub down, cradling it in her arms and suckling it for up to half an hour at a time, six to fourteen times a day. When one breast is exhausted she will move it with nose and paws to the other.

The progress of an infant panda takes the following course:

1 week old The first patches of black appear around the eyes and on the shoulders and ears. At first, the eye patches are round and the cub looks to be wearing sunglasses. It squeals and squeaks a great deal.

2 weeks old The fore and hind legs are now black and the whole coat in general is much thicker. The eye patches have become oblong (the adult shape).

3 weeks old Though the tail is still disproportionately long, the cub now looks like a perfect 'toy' panda. It squeals less.

4 weeks old It now has typical markings, but the tail is still too long. Its eyes are not yet open but are sensitive to light.

5–6 weeks old The eyes are partially open.

6–7 weeks old The eyes are fully open, but its sight is not very good. The cub is able to raise its head and crawl, though only in a very wobbly fashion. It now suckles seven to ten times a day.

10–11 weeks old The cub takes its first shakey steps and its milk teeth appear.

When the cub is between 4 and 7 weeks of age the mother leaves her den and takes the still helpless baby with her, held in her mouth or occasionally tucked under her armpit.

About 3 months old (approx. 5 kg/11 lb) The cub now walks quite well for short distances and its inquisitiveness is evident. It suckles two to three times daily, often while sitting or lying on its back.

About 4 months old (approx. 8–9 kg/$17^1/2$–$19^3/4$ lb) It begins to play a lot, but stays close to its mother.

About 5 months old (approx. 10 kg/22 lb) It can run for short distances and is keen to play, particularly with its mother. It suckles one to two times daily.

About 6 months old (approx. 12–13 kg/$26^1/2$–$28^1/2$ lb) The cub begins to eat solids.

About 8 months old The cub is fully weaned.

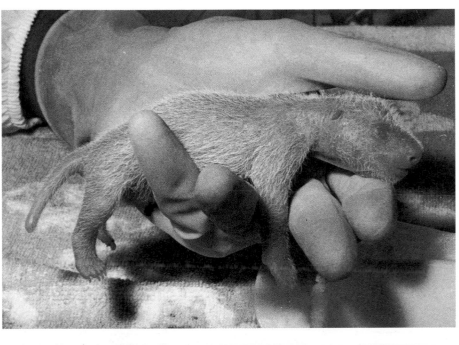

A giant panda cub a few hours after birth at Madrid zoo; it is no larger than a human hand and has very little hair. (J.M. Martos)

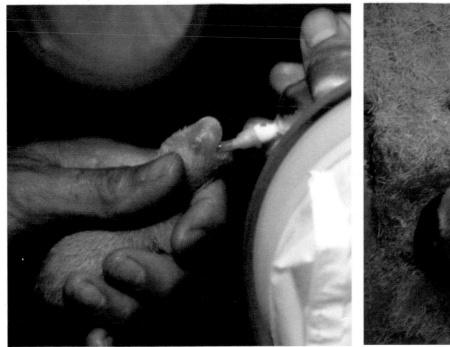

A giant panda is bottle fed at one day old. When twin cubs are born, in nature the smaller one is usually neglected. In a zoo environment, it can be reared by hand if necessary. (J. Knight)

The tiny pink panda cub, shown here just above its mother, is remarkably disproportionate in size to the adult panda in comparison with the young of other species. (J. Knight)

At two weeks the cub has developed a full coat and the typical black and white markings of the giant panda. Here it moves close to its mother's fur and the heat of her body. (J.M. Martos)

A typical posture for the mother to take when suckling her young. (J.M. Martos)

The young cub squeaks and squeals a great deal
during its first two weeks of life. (J.M. Martos)

The small cub is dependent on its mother for many weeks. In her natural habitat the mother would rear her cub in a sheltered cave or hollow tree-trunk den. (J.M. Martos)

In the first month of its life, the cub has difficulty in crawling but does attempt some independent movement. (J.M. Martos)

One month old – and growing fast.
(J.M. Martos)

The mother grooms her cub by carefully licking it clean. (J.M. Martos)

Even at two months old, when the cub is not asleep, it spends most of its time suckling. (J.M. Martos)

At three months old and about 5 kg (11 lb) in weight, the cub can now move independently with confidence and can walk short distances. (J.M. Martos)

At three months old, the growing cub suckles
two or three times each day. (J.M. Martos)

The panda cub becomes increasingly inquisitive
now that it can explore the pen on its own.
(J.M. Martos)

**At almost four months old, the cub plays a lot
but stays close to its mother. (J.M. Martos)**

The cub is almost four months old and weighs
around 9 kg (18 lb). Its curiosity grows and here
can be seen playing with a piece of bamboo.
(J.M. Martos)

At four and a half months old, the cub suckles twice daily but is not yet entirely ready to move on to solid foods. (J.M. Martos)

The cub becomes more playful and at around
six months more games are invented; here it
rolls on the grass in the fresh air at Madrid Zoo.
(J.M. Martos)

The cub, now quite large, plays tumbling games with its mother who is ever good-natured and often joins in, as can be seen overleaf. (J.M. Martos)

Just as the cub's ability to move and play on its
own increases, so does its independence – it is
now able to feed on solid food alone.
(J.M. Martos)

REPRODUCTION IN THE PANDA

As in other species, mothers are tolerant of energetic and mischievous games.
(J.M. Martos)

Lesser panda twins at three months old. It is usual for a litter to contain up to four cubs. (J.M. Martos)

The weaned youngster stays with its parent until it is about $1^1/_2$ years old but, before departing for good, it may leave the maternal range from time to time to hunt for a suitable territory of its own.

When a female panda successfully raises a cub, lactation suppresses her oestrus during the next mating season, and she will not mate again until the year after that, when the youngster has left her. Thus, all being well, a female can produce one cub every 2 years. However, if a cub is lost for any reason during the suckling period, the female can become pregnant again the following spring.

A considerable number of young pandas perish before reaching $2^1/_2$ years of age. Cubs up to 7 weeks old may be taken from their dens by yellow-throated martens or foxes. Some become lost in dense areas of bamboo, or are abandoned when their mother is disturbed or attacked. Others fall victim to leopards, wolves, red dogs or golden cats.

Young pandas up to 4 or 5 years of age are fun-loving, playful creatures who delight in rolling in the grass and tobogganing down snow slopes. Beyond 5 years they become more sober and serious. They can normally expect to reach the ripe old age of about 20–25, and during her lifetime a female may, with a little luck, raise eight or even nine cubs.

Like the giant panda, the lesser panda chooses a dry, hollow tree trunk to use as a cubbing den. After a gestation period of $3^1/_2$ to 5 months (the phenomenon of delayed implantation also occurs in the lesser panda),

A lesser panda cub – its small size is illustrated here by the comparison with the human hands. (J.M. Martos)

between one to four cubs are born. This generally takes place in the month of June, the warm monsoon time of year when the mother is better employed tending her young indoors than getting regularly drenched outside. The cubs enter the world fully-furred, blind, helpless and weighing 105–130 g (3^1/$_2$–4^1/$_2$ oz). It takes 2 to 4 weeks for their eyes to open. They suckle from their mother for 4 to 5 months and become sexually mature at around 20 months of age. Their life expectancy is 13 to 14 years.

7

THE PANDA'S FUTURE

Everything has its beauty but not everyone sees it.
CONFUCIUS, *ANALECTS*

The giant panda, unique in many ways and one of our rarest mammals, is protected by both Chinese and international laws. Nevertheless as the twentieth century draws to a close, threats to its survival persist. If its fate is not to be the same as that of the dodo or Steller's sea-cow, animals gone for ever not as a result of natural evolutionary forces but because of man's lethal influence on the environment, these threats must be identified and neutralized.

We know from the fossil records that during the Pleistocene epoch giant pandas were widely distributed across China. During the ice ages of this epoch the bamboo died back and the panda population shrank; between them, the climate warmed up, the glaciers melted, and both bamboo and pandas flourished. When the Holocene epoch, 'modern times', dawned around 50,000 years ago, the panda was still relatively common in much of China and parts of Burma. The climate was more or less stable and, being warm and wet, was ideal for bamboo.

The past 2,000 years have been somewhat cooler and dryer, but not to a degree sufficient to cause significant decline in the bamboo or the panda that lives on it. However, over the past 2,000 years, and particularly in the past 200 years, man rather than the climate has been responsible for the steady dwindling of the panda's numbers. As the human population grew apace in provinces such as Szechuan, so that of the panda contracted.

It is really a pity the education of the human species did not develop in time to save the irremediable destruction of so many species which the Creator placed on earth to live beside man, not merely for beauty, but to fulfil a useful role necessary for the economy of the whole. A selfish and blind preoccupation with material interests has caused us to reduce this cosmos, so marvellous to him with eyes to see it, to a hard, matter-of-fact place. Soon the horse and the pig on one hand and wheat and potatoes on the other will replace hundreds of thousands of animals and plants given us by God.

FROM THE DIARY OF PÈRE DAVID

Snug in the undergrowth, a young cub chews on a tender stem. (Ardea/Keith & Liz Laidler)

The Wolong Valley where one of the large nature and wildlife conservation centres is located. The terracing that can be seen here on the hill ridges indicates the agricultural development from which the panda research station aims to shelter the pandas within its confines. (J. Knight)

The giant panda population, distributed between twelve reserves in six separate areas in central China, cannot be precisely calculated, though censuses have been attempted. It is possibly in the region of 500, and is certainly no more than 1,000. This remarkable species, which has been in existence for 3 million years longer than *Homo sapiens*, has never before been reduced to such perilously low numbers.

Following large-scale deaths of giant pandas in the late 1970s after the flowering of bamboo in many parts of the animals' range in north Szechuan, the World Wide Fund for Nature met with the Academia Sinica, the Chinese Association for Environmental Sciences and the Chinese Ministry of Forestry to formulate a plan for conservation of the species. For 30 years up to that time the Chinese had been making observations on and conducting censuses of the pandas, but it was now considered essential that a programme of international scientific cooperation be established without delay in order to avert what might already be an accelerating decline towards extinction. The outcome was the formation, in 1979, of the China-WWF Joint Committee which at once set about the construction of a research centre on the giant panda (at Wolong) and a number of monitoring stations as the beginning of a three-pronged research programme which would aim to study all aspects of wild panda populations, investigate nutrition, reproduction and health care under captive conditions, and draw up an Emergency Plan to cope with any future natural disasters.

The research centre in the Wolong Valley.
(J. Knight)

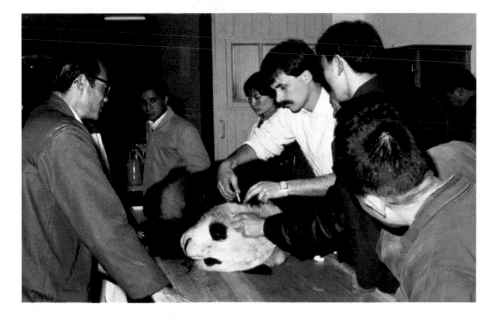

Chinese vets and scientists work alongside
visitors from other countries and together they
work towards a better understanding of the
giant panda. (J. Knight)

Foreign scientists, from the USA in particular, came to work on the
various projects in collaboration with their Chinese counterparts and the
impressive results of the first few years of work were published in 1985
(*The giant pandas of Wolong*: George B. Schaller, Hu Jinchu, Pan Wenshi
and Zhu Jing).

The largest of the twelve remaining populations, that of the Wolong
Nature Reserve, consists of fewer than 150 animals, and even these are
split up into fairly discrete sub-groups. Half to two-thirds of all the pandas
are to be found in those reserves which cover a total of some 600,000 hectares (1.5 million acres). This gives an average of one panda to between 3
and 10 sq km (1–4 sq miles), depending upon the suitability of the terrain
and its bamboo cover.

Monitoring the daily life of pandas in their rugged and beautiful home territory is a difficult task. The animals can be tracked, either by means of radio-telemetry after trapping them humanely in log traps with sliding doors and baits of cooked meat, tranquillizing them briefly and fitting a collar bearing a small but powerful radio transmitter around their necks, or by following the trail of their droppings. Experienced 'dung detectors' can tell the age of a panda by scrutinizing its faeces. For example,

droppings of a young panda are about $3^{1}/_{2}$ cms. in diameter, while those of an old individual measure $6–6^{1}/_{2}$ cms. The direction of travel can also be gleaned from this excremental evidence for, as we have seen, the panda has the habit of defecating regularly while on the move. It so happens that the narrower end of a panda stool points in the direction that the animal has gone!

One of the fundamental questions in the conservation of the panda is: at what point does a diminishing population become unviable? What is the critical number below which it cannot sustain itself and is inevitably doomed? Some experts suggest that, in the case of the panda, the minimum population necessary to ensure long-term survival is as many as 50, possibly even 100 animals. Nine of the twelve panda reserves currently contain less than 50, and three of these contain less than 20.

Pandas are slow reproducers, and although they are cocooned by laws and regulations, and inhabit a remote part of the country that lacks both predators and competitors for food, they do face a number of perils. With their numbers so low, every panda lost, for whatever reason, assumes an even greater significance for the chances of survival of the species.

Pandas are killed, usually as juveniles, by leopards, bears, red dogs and the like, while others die in traps set for deer, in natural disasters (such as the severe earthquake that struck Szechuan in 1976), and, despite the harsh penalties for offenders, at the hands of illegal hunters. In March 1990, two men were publicly executed in Mianyang, Szechuan, for trafficking in panda skins.

As we went along the ridge we saw two spear traps the house owner had used for killing pandas . . . The construction was simple and interesting: the principle was simply that of a heavy spruce sapling laid horizontally about two feet above the ground with its base bound to another tree. At right angles to the top was attached a strong piece of bamboo with an iron point securely fastened. Once set the point of the latter was just beside the trail; it took the strength of two men to pull the sapling back where it was set with a figure-four arrangement and a string across the trail; if tripped by an animal this very lethal spear would be released impaling an animal chest high.

WILLIAM SHELDON, *THE WILDERNESS HOME OF THE GIANT PANDA*
Sheldon was an American hunter who went in search of the panda in 1934 and shot one in December of that year. Spear traps of the kind described are now illegal in panda country.

The lesser panda is also well protected by the laws of China, India and Nepal, but some illegal hunting still takes place. Sadly, one lesser panda pelt makes a fine fur hat.

The smaller the population of pandas in any given zone, the more risk there is of in-breeding and the long-term, weakening effect which that has on the species. Pandas are often heavily infested with intestinal worms. Like other wild animals, they are normally able to co-exist comfortably with their burden of free-loading parasites, but if they are squeezed into ever smaller areas of land it may result in a dramatic multiplication of their worms. If the territory available to a given number of animals for foraging is halved, the number of parasites taken in by them *quadruples* and can eventually reach the point where illness and even death occur.

However, the major threat to both the giant and the lesser panda is the change in their habitat, the bamboo forest on which they so intimately

> **Losang and her three sisters**
>
> In Tibet there is a version of the legend, recounted in the Introduction, about how the giant panda acquired its unique markings. The heroic girl, say the Tibetans, was a shepherdess by the name of Losang and she had three sisters. After their deaths they were turned into mountains, the 'Four Girls Peaks' which rise today just to the north-west of the giant panda reserve at Wolong.

rely. China's teeming human population exerts ever-growing pressure on the country's natural resources. The forests of the panda homelands are a mixture of bamboo and many species of tree and shrub. Man has moved gradually but inexorably into the mountain forests – up to 10,000 peasants live in seven of the twelve panda reserves – converting the lower slopes in many places into fields for crops or livestock, and higher up taking bamboo for domestic use and hard woods for the state timber industry.

All kinds of tree are logged, not just for their value as wood, but for other products as well; laurel for perfume, Chinese walnut for tannin, for example. The vine's edible underground stems are rich in starch; they are also used to make rope and medicines, and for the extraction of aromatic oils. Most important of all to the logging industry are the conifers at an altitude of between 2,500 and 3,500 m (8,200–11,500 ft). These provide a major source of timber for construction as well as providing the raw material for paper and rayon.

This clump contains both living and dead bamboo side by side. The pandas must separate the nutritious crop from the dying stems in order to find enough to eat. (J. Knight)

Logging removes the canopy of high trees that shades the bamboo. This exposes the bamboo to increased sunlight, with the result that it grows much more densely, is less accessible, and appears less palatable to the pandas. In turn, these close-packed thickets of bamboo smother the growth of tree seedlings and so the mixed forest is incapable of regenerating itself.

We know that pandas eat different species of bamboo at different times of the year. In most of the panda reserves, *Sinarundinaria* is not, as yet, declining. However, the *Fargesia*, whose shoots are so important to the animals in spring, is diminishing, due partly to insect attack, but mainly to the pandas' attentions in recent years. When the *Sinarundinaria* flowered and died back in the early 1980s, hungry pandas ate more *Fargesia*, and their habit of browsing round the borders of the stands and selecting thick shoots has hampered the natural growth and spread of the plant more than in the past. Scientists are not sure how long the flowering interval may be in *Fargesia*, but some records suggest that it could be as much as ninety-nine years. We know it flowered in many places in the 1890s, so it is more than possible that, at some time in the next few years, *Fargesia* will burst into bloom again, and the pandas will once more be threatened by a bamboo famine.

The Giant Panda is our national treasure. We should make friends with it. How could I drive it away?

LI HUAXAN, A SZECHUAN PEASANT INTO WHOSE HUT A PANDA WALKED ONE DAY IN 1983.

Reforestation is an important part of conservation. If young trees are planted then it may eventually be possible for pandas to return to live in areas that they used to inhabit in earlier times. (J. Knight)

What, then, are the measures being taken to alleviate some of these threats to the giant panda's survival? Apart from establishing the twelve panda reserves, with the possibility of more in the future, the Chinese government has set up a number of research and monitoring programmes to gain more vital information on the population dynamics of the species. In some places, communes and farms close to the panda forests are being moved and resettled; electricity supplies are being extended and financial help given in insulating dwellings with the aim of reducing demand for firewood; and bamboo-cutting has been prohibited.

Pandas and man

From time to time remarkable encounters between men and pandas have been recorded.

In October 1978 a sick panda walked into a peasant commune where a family fed it on rice gruel and sugar-cane for three days until, looking considerably fitter, it went on its way.

In 1982 a weak lost or orphaned panda cub was found by a peasant and taken to the nearest village, where it was carefully nursed back to health. The cub, given the name 'Xiao Le' ('Little Happiness'), tamed quickly and learned to stretch out one of its forepaws to be shaken when greeted with the words 'How do you do, Xiao Le?'

In September 1983 a panda entered the hut of a peasant, Li Huax-uan, in a lacquer tree forest while Li was inside. Virtually ignoring Li, the panda ate a bowl of cooked rice and then jumped onto the wooden bed or Kang. After spending some time shredding the sleeping quilt to its satisfaction, it rested for a while before leaving.

In February 1984 a panda that had fallen into a partially iced-over river and found itself in difficulties was rescued by three girls out collecting firewood. They jumped into the freezing water to save it, and then lit a fire to dry it off while other peasants brought bamboo branches, boiled rice, meat and sugar, on which it fed before returning to the forest.

In Spring, 1972 a group of Chinese zoologists out tracking pandas in the Houjiagou forest came across an adult male napping in a cave. It woke up when the men entered its grotto but showed no sign of being in the slightest perturbed. One of the scientists cautiously went up to it and scratched it gently, first with a bamboo twig and then with his hand. The panda evidently enjoyed the experience, for it turned one way and then another in order to have its back, sides and stomach tickled. Gifts of bamboo were eagerly accepted by the animal which seemed content to let the humans go out to gather stems and leaves for it. It ate its fill, slept and then ate its fill again and by the end of a 24 hour period it had scoffed 76 kg of bamboo. The monitoring team spent two days in the cave waiting upon the panda before it moved out. The following year, the same zoologists had a similar experience with another panda, and on that occasion spent three days bivouacked with what appeared to be another remarkably affable individual.

A giant panda is transported back to the wild after spending a short time under observation at a research station. (Rex Features)

Peasants are being encouraged, often with the aid of cash incentives, to protect and care for the forest flora and fauna, and fields are being re-converted into woodland by planting trees and bamboo.

Rescue stations with veterinary hospital facilities, laboratories and breeding units, have been built and staffed by teams whose duties include finding and bringing in starving pandas. Sometimes pandas have been translocated under sedation from areas where the bamboo has flowered to others where it has not. Supplementary foods, such as grain, sugar-cane and meat are put out in the forest as and when necessary, and rewards are given by the state to individuals who help any pandas that find themselves in difficulties.

Obviously the planting of bamboo, particularly on denuded lower mountain slopes, is a priority and this work will be greatly accelerated by recent research in India, where scientists have shown that bamboo shoots which would not normally flower until they were about 30 years of age, can be made to do so in *2 weeks* by feeding them on a cocktail of coconut milk, plant hormones and other nutrients. This discovery is of the utmost importance, for it will facilitate the breeding of new varieties of bamboo, and will enable much faster replacement of depleted forests than has hith-erto been possible. When replanting bamboo, the Chinese are taking care to ensure that at least *two* varieties are used, as a precaution against the day that one or other flowers.

Another project being considered by the Chinese government is the linking of some of the twelve panda reserves by bamboo corridors planted in the intervening countryside. These would enable the animals to travel and mix, so diminishing the risks of interbreeding, and allowing them to explore other food sources when the need arises.

Pandas in captivity

In about the year 200 BC, at the beginning of the Han Dynasty, a new palace was built by the emperor in a suburb of Xian, the then capital. In its vast grounds was a zoo, the Shanglin Garden, surrounded by 100 km of wall and containing a collection of all manner of animals, not only for the emperor to admire, but also for him to hunt when the fancy took him. The writer, Sima Xiangru (179–117 BC) in his essay, *Song to Shanglin*, declared that 'of all the birds and animals in the Shanglin Garden, *mo* (the giant panda) is the loveliest'.

Meanwhile, there is a role for the study and breeding of giant pandas in the major zoological collections in China and the select group of other countries to which pairs have been sent, as political presents, since 1955. So far the breeding record of these animals outside China has not, on the whole, been very impressive. One reason for this may be that 'arranged marriages' do not allow for the hierarchical social structure, rare meet-ings, and mate selection rituals enjoyed by pandas in the wild.

In order to observe the panda more closely, scientists will often spend time living near to the animals on the mountainside, sleeping and working in tents on specially constructed platforms. (Rex Features)

Nevertheless, following the first successful zoo birth, at Beijing Zoo in 1963, over eighty pandas have been bred in zoos in China, and others in Mexico, Japan and Spain, with about 30 per cent surviving to at least one year of age. In 1978, again in Beijing, the first successful birth resulting from artificial insemination was achieved. And in 1982, 'Shao-Shoa', one of the pandas at the Zoo de la Casa de Campo, Madrid, for which I am particularly responsible, was inseminated with semen flown over from London Zoo's male, 'Chia-Chia'. The 'test-tube' cub that was born as a result, and named 'Chu-Lin' ('Treasure among the Bamboos') is a happy, healthy 8-year-old as I write.

Much research has been, and continues to be, carried out on pandas both in their native forests and in zoos. In the wild we need to know far more about the animal's delicate interaction with its habitat, the factors that are involved in maintaining a viable, healthy population, the ways of expanding suitable bamboo-forest reserves and of re-introducing the species into areas where it once lived.

In the zoo we constantly study the health, nutrition and reproduction of the panda, gathering information that can help in the rescue of sick and starving pandas, their rehabilitation, and the setting up of breeding programmes and genetic pools in the form of sperm and embryo banks.

The fate of the giant panda is still in the balance, but I believe that the efforts of the Chinese government and people, cooperating increasingly now with scientists from overseas, will with a little *feng-shui* (luck) be rewarded, and that they will succeed in preserving this most wondrous of creatures, a prime example of wildlife conservation at its best, for generations to come.

The giant panda as we would hope to see it – in a world where its future is increasingly protected. (Rex Features)

SUGGESTIONS FOR FURTHER READING

David, A., *Abbé David's Diary* (1874) translated by H.M. Fox; Harvard University Press, 1946.

Davis, J., *Pandas*; Curtis Books, 1973.

Ewer, R., *The Carnivores*; George Weidenfeld and Nicholson, 1973.

Harkness, R., *The Lady and the Panda*; Nicholson & Watson, 1938.

Ma, X. and Tang, G., *Giant Panda's Habitat*; Dolphin Books, 1988.

Macdonald, D., *The Encyclopaedia of Mammals: 1*; Allen & Unwin, 1984.

Morris, R. and Morris, D., *Men and Pandas*; Hutchinson, 1966; revised edition, Kogan Page, 1981.

Roosevelt, T. and Roosevelt, K., *Trailing the Giant Panda*; Scribner's, 1929.

Schaller, G., Hu, J., Pan, W. and Zhu, J., *The Giant Pandas of Wolong*; University of Chicago Press, 1985.

Sheldon, W., *The Wilderness Home of the Giant Panda*; University of Massachussetts Press, 1975.

Taylor, D., *Next Panda Please*; Allen & Unwin, 1982.

Taylor, D., *Vet on the Wild Side*; Robson Books, 1990.

Zhu, J. and Li, Y., *The Giant Panda*; Science Press, Beijing, 1980.

Anon, *The Giant Panda*; China Pictorial, Beijing, 1984.

INDEX

PICTURE CREDITS

The publishers and author would like to thank the following sources for use of the photographs on pages listed:

Front jacket picture NHPA, back jacket picture Bruce Coleman/WWF/Kojo Tanaka
page 9 NHPA/Gérard Lacz
page 11 J.M. Martos
page 12 John Knight
page 13 J.M. Martos
page 14 J.M. Martos
page 16 Mary Evans Picture Library
page 19 J.M. Martos
page 20/21 Survival Anglia/Des & Jen Bartlett
page 21 John Knight
page 22/23 Bruce Coleman/Gerald Cubitt
page 29 Bruce Coleman/WWF/Kojo Tanaka
page 30 Survival Anglia/Jeff Foott
page 31 J.M. Martos
page 32 Bruce Coleman/WWF/Kojo Tanaka
page 34 Bruce Coleman/WWF/Timm Rautert
page 35 J.M. Martos
page 36 John Knight
page 37 John Knight
page 38 J.M. Martos
page 39 J.M. Martos
page 41 Rex Features
page 43 John Knight
page 45 John Knight
page 46 John Knight
page 47 Ardea/Joanna Van Gruisen
page 48 Ardea/Kenneth W. Fink
page 49 Ardea/Joanna Van Gruisen
page 50 Ardea/Kenneth W. Fink
page 51 Ardea/Wardene Weisser
page 52 Ardea/Kenneth W. Fink
page 53 Ardea/Kenneth W. Fink
page 54 Ardea/Stefan Meyers
page 57 John Knight
page 58 Rex Features/Peter Brooker
page 59 John Knight
page 60 NHPA/Philippa Scott
page 63 John Knight
page 64 Rex Features
page 65 John Knight
page 67 Bruce Coleman/WWF/Kojo Tanaka
page 68/69 Bruce Coleman/WWF/Kojo Tanaka
page 70 Bruce Coleman/WWF/Kojo Tanaka
page 71 John Knight
page 72/73 Bruce Coleman/WWF/Timm Rautert
page 75 John Knight

page 76 Rex Features
page 78/79 Bruce Coleman/WWF/Timm Rautert
page 81 Bruce Coleman/WWF/Timm Rautert
page 82 Bruce Coleman/WWF/Kojo Tanaka
page 83 John Knight
page 85 Rex Features
page 86/87 Survival Anglia/Dieter & Mary Plage
page 88/89 Bruce Coleman/WWF/Timm Rautert
page 91 J.M. Martos
page 92 John Knight
page 93 John Knight
page 94 John Knight
page 95 John Knight
page 96 J.M. Martos
page 97 John Knight
page 98–123 J.M. Martos
page 125 Ardea/Keith & Liz Laidler
page 126 John Knight
page 127 John Knight
page 128 J.M. Martos
page 128/129 Rex Features
page 131 John Knight
page 132 John Knight
page 134/135 Rex Features
page 136/137 Rex Features
page 138/139 Rex Features